Test your Psychic Powers

Once a parapsychologist, **Susan Blackmore** has researched the psychic world from astral projection to Zener cards and written numerous books on out-of-body experiences, memes, meditation and consciousness. She is a freelance writer, TED lecturer, and Visiting Professor in Psychology at the University of Plymouth, UK.

Adam Hart-Davis spent 30 years in television, producing Arthur C Clarke's World of Strange Powers, and presenting Local Heroes, Tomorrow's World, What the Romans (and others) Did for Us, and many others. He has collected awards for both television and radio, and has written more than 30 books, mainly about science, technology, and history.

Selected Titles by the Authors:
Susan Blackmore:
Zen and the Art of Consciousness (Oneworld Publications, 2011)
Consciousness: An Introduction (Hodder Education, 2010)
Conversations on Consciousness (Oxford University Press, 2005)
A Very Short Introduction to Consciousness (Oxford University Press, 2005)
The Meme Machine (Oxford University Press, 1999)
In Search of the Light: The Adventures of a Parapsychologist (Prometheus Books, 1996)
Dying to Live: Science and the Near Death Experience, (Grafton, 1993)
Beyond the Body: An investigation into out-of-body experiences (William Heinemann 1982/1992)

Adam Hart-Davis
History: From the Dawn of Civilization to the Present Day - (Dorling Kindersley, 3rd Edition, 2015)
The Science Book - BIG Ideas Simply Explained (Dorling Kindersley, 2014)
The Book of Time (Mitchell Beazley, 2011)
Engineers (Dorling Kindersley, 2011)
Science: The Definitive Visual Guide (Dorling Kindersley, 2009)
The Cosmos: A Beginner's Guide (BBC Books, 2007)
Just Another Day: The Science and Technology of Our Everyday Lives (Orion, 2006)
Why Does A Ball Bounce? And 100 Other Questions from the World of Science (Ebury, 2005)
What the Past Did For Us (BBC Books, 2004)
What the Tudors and Stuarts Did For Us (BBC Books, 2002)
What the Victorians Did For Us (Headline, 2001)
Pavlov's Dog (Metro Books, 2015)
Schrodinger's Cat (Metro Books, 2015)

Test your Psychic Powers

■ ■ ■

Susan Blackmore and Adam Hart-Davis

Thorsons
An Imprint of HarperCollins*Publishers*

Dedicated to Dinky

Contents

Introduction

Many people believe in psychic powers. Even if they can't themselves dowse, or see the future, they are convinced that other people can. Vast numbers of people look at their horoscopes in the paper on the way to work every day. Most of us are only too willing to have 'sensitive' people read our palms—and perhaps our minds.

In this book, each chapter focuses on one of the alleged psychic powers, starting with telepathy and going through to palmistry and astrology.

New Age claims may or may not be true. This book does not pretend to give you all the answers, but aims to encourage you to experience New Age sensations, and explains how to use scientific methods to try and reach the truth. Whether or not you believe in the paranormal processes sometimes called 'psi', the phenomena are fascinating both to experience and to test for yourself.

We have all had the experience of thinking about someone when the phone rings—and it's the self-same person on the line. Is that telepathy, or just coincidence? In the first chapter you will read the most amazing telepathy stories of all time, and then take a rational look at the phenomenon. How can it work? Can the claims be tested? Are you yourself telepathic?

Go ahead, dip in. And do try some of the experiments. See whether you can change your dreams, or influence woodlice by mind-power. We hope you will have as much fun doing the tests as we have had in thinking them up and trying them out. The great advantage of carrying out the experiments yourself is that if you are careful enough in your procedure, you can be sure of the results.

Good luck!

Susan Blackmore
Adam Hart-Davis

Bristol, April 1995

1

Telepathy

People have always wanted a sixth sense – an extra channel of communication that might help in emergency, or just be fun and baffling to others. We all get occasional glimpses of this: the phone rings – and you know who is calling before you pick it up; or during a conversation a particular phrase comes to you – and as you open your mouth to say it, someone else says exactly the same thing.

Telepathy means direct communication from one mind to another, and is one of the best-known forms of extra-sensory perception, or ESP. But does it really happen – or is it only wishful thinking? Because we would *like* telepathy to be true, we find it hard to be objective about the phenomenon, and often think it must be real even when there is no proof. However, there are a few cases in which the evidence is strong – and there seems to have been genuine mind-to-mind communication.

On her Way to the Movies

One afternoon in 1955, Joicey Hurth was washing the dishes in the kitchen of her white wooden house in Cedarburg, Wisconsin, when her husband and young son came in and said they were going off to see a Walt Disney film at the Rivoli Cinema in the main street.

Five minutes later her daughter, little Joicey, came back from a birthday party and was sad to find that the others had gone to the cinema without her; she wanted to go, too. Her mother said, 'Why don't you run along and join them? Just be careful crossing the street.' So young Joicey skipped off up the road.

It wasn't long before a sudden dreadful chill came over her mother. She said later that she froze, dropped the dish she was washing, raised her eyes to heaven and said, 'Please don't let her get killed!' She did not know what had happened; she did not hear or see anything; she just had a *feeling* there had been some sort of accident, that something had happened to her daughter.

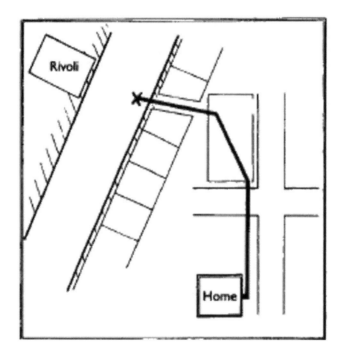

Figure 1.1: Little Joicey's route to the cinema in Cedarburg, Wisconsin.

She stepped across the kitchen, picked up the phone and rang the Rivoli. A young woman answered and Joicey stammered, 'Get me the manager…please.'

The manager came on the line, and Joicey said, 'My daughter's had an accident. Is she badly hurt?'

Ray Nichols was astounded. He stammered, too: 'Mrs Hurth, it…the accident…it only just happened. Your daughter's OK; she doesn't seem to be badly hurt. Your husband is with her now.'

Little Joicey had walked about 300 yards, along a route that was well out of sight and earshot of her home, to the cinema on a different street.

She had walked 100 yards up the road, over an intersection, diagonally across a car park and between two buildings down a narrow passage which came out directly across the road from the cinema. Unfortunately she had run out of this passage without looking, straight in front of a car. She wasn't badly hurt but she had got a nasty shock. She sat down on the kerb, saying, 'Momma, Momma, I want my Momma' – but just to herself, not out loud.

The people in the cinema saw the accident happen, called her father and ran to help the little girl on the pavement.

Joicey's telephone call came through as her husband reached their daughter.

Ray Nichols was still amazed when I talked to him 30 years later. 'If I'd had a motorbike standing by, I couldn't have got the news to her so quickly,' he said. 'It had to be extra-sensory perception. It had to be. There's no other way.'

Midwife in Need

The winter of 1952 was cold and miserable in Norfolk; snow lay on the ground for weeks, and midwife Gladys Wright had a terrible time reaching her patients in the scattered rural community – for in those days, in England, most babies were born at home, and she had to be there to deliver them.

One date she will never forget is 15th December of that year. Gales had brought down the telephone lines; so all the phones were out of action. She had no means of finding out what was going on. None of her patients was due to have a baby for several days, but during the course of the afternoon Gladys began to worry about one of them, and eventually became convinced that Mrs Goodwin wanted her ... needed her.

While she and her husband were eating their evening meal, she told him about her feeling. He told her not to worry and said that they would send for her if they needed her. But even though Mrs Goodwin's baby was not due until 23rd December, eight days ahead, Gladys felt sure it was on its way.

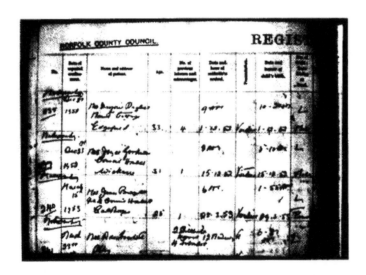

Figure 1.2: A page from Gladys Wright's register of cases. Mrs Goodwin's baby was delivered at five in the morning, eight days early.

Eventually she went to bed at about 10.30, but Gladys could not sleep. She tossed and turned, and turned and tossed, with this feeling in her mind growing stronger and stronger until at last, long after midnight, she woke her husband and said 'It's no good; I'm going to Wickmere!' He was annoyed: 'Then you're a blithering idiot!' But she ignored him, got up, collected her medical bag and set off in her car through the white winter night.

She slithered all over the road for four miles, and began to feel an awful fool as she approached Wickmere. What would the Goodwins say if she turned up at 2 a.m. and they were all asleep? She decided she would simply turn round and go quietly home, and never tell a soul.

But when she arrived the house was all lit up. She ran up the garden path and found Joyce Goodwin leaning on the kitchen table, already in strong labour. Baby Steven was born at 5.10 a.m., and Joyce Goodwin still remembers how glad she was to see Mrs Wright. 'I really wanted you to come, but didn't know how to call you – and then you walked in out of the blue ... well, out of the snow, I suppose!'

One thing these stories have in common is that there was a crisis: one person was in trouble and the other seemed to sense it from a distance. Sometimes a crisis can lead to what psychical researchers have called a 'crisis apparition', as in this next case.

The Hospital Gown

Pat and Shirley had been friends for years. One night in 1975 Pat woke in her home in Essex to hear her name being called. At the bottom of her bed she saw the head and shoulders of her friend Shirley, who looked haggard and seemed to be in pain. What struck Pat most forcibly, however, was that Shirley was wearing something she wouldn't normally be seen dead in.

Shirley was always a snappy dresser, and yet here she was in a shapeless cotton top with square shoulders and a ragged neck... Pat was so surprised by this that she drew a sketch of the garment – like a T-shirt with a torn ragged neck.

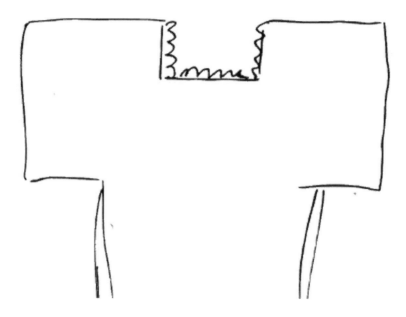

Figure 1.3: Pat's sketch of the shapeless garment she saw Shirley wearing, in her vision.

In the morning she tried to phone Shirley, but got no reply. What she did not know was that Shirley had gone with her husband on holiday to Mombasa, Kenya – 4,000 miles away. While she was there she had had a minor accident and had had to go into hospital for a small operation on her Achilles tendon.

For this operation the hospital staff had given her a shapeless cotton hospital gown, with a ragged neck.

When Shirley returned to England and she and Pat spoke on the phone, the first thing Pat asked her was, 'Whatever happened to you?' When they got together, Shirley confirmed that the hospital gown was just like the one in the sketch Pat had drawn.

The Scientific Approach to ESP

The main evidence for ESP – the main reason why so many people believe it happens – is that we hear such powerful anecdotes and stories, which psychical researchers call 'spontaneous cases'. Joicey Hurth did not send her daughter deliberately out into the busy traffic; the extraordinary message came in response to a spontaneous event.

In the 1920s and 1930s science was striding forward. Albert Einstein was a popular and respected man, even if hardly anyone really understood his ideas. To have a scientific approach was sensible and respectable – and many people began trying to apply science to telepathy, and to do deliberate experiments to see whether messages could be conveyed without using the five normal senses.

Mary Craig Sinclair's 'Mental Radio'

Mary Craig was born in Mississippi in the 1880s, and had several spiritual and 'psychic' experiences in her early life. She married journalist and novelist Upton Sinclair, and from about 1928 conducted with him a long series of drawing experiments which he then collected and described in the book *Mental Radio.* This is a typical experiment from the book:

> Upton went into his study. 'I was alone, and the door was closed before the drawing was made, and was not opened until the test was concluded. Having made the drawing, I held it before me and concentrated upon it for a period of five or ten minutes.
>
> '...My wife...was lying on the couch in her study, about 30 feet away from me, with the door closed

between us. The only words spoken were as follows: when I was ready to make my drawing, I called, "All right," and when she had completed her drawings, she called, "All right." '

He had drawn a six-pointed star. She also drew a six-pointed star. The similarity between the figures was remarkable. Mary managed to perform this sort of impressive feat dozens of times, with various senders, and said she saw the pictures by a sort of 'mental radio'. As her husband says in his book, 'if X-rays leave a permanent record on metal, why might not brain-rays, or thought-rays, leave a record on a piece of paper? Why might not such energies be reflected back to another brain, as light is reflected by a mirror?'

Figure 1.4: Mental radio? (a) Upton Sinclair's drawing and (b) Mary Craig Sinclair's drawing. They had drawn them in separate rooms.

Joseph Banks Rhine

J. B. Rhine was trained as a botanist, but in 1922 he heard an inspiring lecture given by Sir Arthur Conan Doyle promoting psychical research and spiritualism. A few years later he gave up his career in botany and embarked on a study of psychical research. After a dreadful experience with the famous medium Margery Crandon, he decided that he would take his research out of the seance room and into the laboratory, and make it an experimental science – parapsychology.

In 1927 he secured a position at Duke University in North Carolina, and there with the help of his wife Louisa he began to put ESP on the scientific map. He seems to have coined the expression 'extra-sensory perception', by which he meant receiving information by some means other than the five normal senses of sight, hearing, touch, taste or smell.

Within this category (ESP), J. B. Rhine included:

- telepathy – direct communication of thoughts from one mind to another
- clairvoyance – the 'seeing' of hidden objects, such as pictures in sealed envelopes
- precognition – seeing the future

He decided to test people for ESP by using cards. In a well-shuffled pack of playing cards no one knows which order to expect. If one person turns them face-up one by one, while another person sits in a different room and guesses the order, then you would expect the guesser to be right occasionally, just by chance. But if the person who turns them over looks hard at each card, and the guesser tries to pick up his or her thoughts, then with help from ESP the guesser should be right more often than would be expected by chance alone.

Regular playing cards have disadvantages. Some are well known, like the ace of spades and the queen of hearts, and many have complicated pictures on the faces. They also vary in design; so someone trying to send a message might be confused by the mass of information. Rhine decided he should use simpler cards, and asked a colleague, Professor

Karl Zener, to design a special pack of cards for testing ESP. Zener cards have been used in such tests ever since. There are five different symbols, designed not to be mystical signs but merely to be easy to recognize and distinguish from each other. The pack contains five cards with each symbol – 25 cards in all.

Figure 1.5: A pack of Zener cards (or ESP cards) consists of 25 cards: 5 each depicting wavy lines, circle, square, cross, and star.

The cards were highly successful, but Rhine's work was so controversial when it was first published in 1934 that

Professor Zener refused to have his name associated with it and the cards had to be renamed ESP cards – at least officially. In fact most people still refer to them as Zener cards in spite of his objections!

Rhine's work was just the beginning of 60 years of research into parapsychology. Many more sophisticated experiments have been carried out and evidence for ESP claimed. However, in spite of all this research there is still no experiment that provides repeatable results, and most scientists remain unconvinced that ESP really exists.

How Might Telepathy Work?

According to most scientific theories, telepathy ought to be impossible. Psychologists take it for granted that we only have five senses, and see no reason to invoke telepathy as well.

If telepathy existed it would violate some simple assumptions of physics in rather dramatic ways. For example, it doesn't seem to matter how far apart the two people are or how many other people there are in between them! The messages seem to be able to go round corners, through walls and under water, and the process is not even strictly tied to time. This may be why its existence is still so controversial even after 100 years of experiments.

There are plenty of theories about telepathy, but none of them is well accepted. The most popular is probably the idea that telepathy works like radio transmission. People often talk of 'vibrations' and 'frequencies' as though there were telepathic 'brain-waves' going from one person to another.

The problem is that if there were some kind of radiation we ought to be able to detect it coming from people's brains, and we cannot. The brain's electrical activity can be detected at best only a few centimeters away from the skull.

There would also need to be a transmitter in one brain and a receiver in the other – and no sign of either has ever been detected. Even worse is that the strength of the signal ought to decay with distance – yet Joicey Hurth was a few hundred yards from her mother and Pat and Shirley were thousands of miles apart. Distance seems to make no difference.

More fanciful theories suggest that there is some other realm – perhaps a thought world, or psychic field – in which the impressions of every thought and emotion are stored. Telepathy would then involve picking up the impressions from this psychic field.

The main problem here is that there is no independent evidence for this psychic field and no easy way to decide whether it exists or not. Also, try to imagine what it would be like if you could pick up impressions from such a 'collective memory'. Wouldn't you get inundated with the thoughts left behind by Julius Caesar, Henry the Eighth and the scullery maid who worked in his kitchen? It is very hard to see how one brain could pick up just those messages it needed and ignore all the rest.

So, does ESP exist? The way to find out is do some scientific experiments.

Telepathy Experiments

Testing yourself and your friends for telepathy can be a lot of fun. We suggest you start with simple tests and then, if you find someone who really seems to have ESP, you can go on to do experiments with proper scientific controls.

Drawing Games

In the early days of psychical research a simple kind of drawing test was popular. You can try it yourself. One person (called the *Sender*) draws a picture of the first thing that comes to mind, then the other (called the *Receiver*) tries to draw the same thing. The early psychical researchers called this 'thought transference'.

You must make sure the Receiver cannot possibly see what the Sender is drawing. You might make them sit back to back, put up a screen between them, or sit them in opposite corners of the room. You might even decide to put them in different rooms.

When both Sender and Receiver have finished, compare the results. You may be surprised by how similar the drawings are – but is this telepathy?

Can you think what is wrong with this as a test?

The most important problem is that 'the first thing that comes to mind' is quite likely to be the same for both people. Everyone tends to draw a house or a boat first time they try the experiment – if only because they are easy to draw! Then the drawings get more subtle. But if the two people know each other well they may still pick the same thing.

For example, you and your friend might both think of drawing an elephant because the Experimenter is called Nell; or a rose because there was a slurpy song on the radio just now; or even a plane because you'd both heard news that morning of a terrible plane crash. Drawing 'the first thing that comes to mind' won't do.

In addition, if you wanted to fool an Experimenter you could both agree beforehand what you were going to draw.

This is why later experiments used playing cards, or the special ESP cards that the Rhines developed. The idea was that if the cards were shuffled and you looked at them one at a time, you could never know in advance what message you had to send. The order of the cards would be random.

Since you can easily get hold of a pack of playing cards, we suggest you use these for your first test. If you take out the court cards (Jacks, Queens, Kings), the most distracting pictures will be gone and you will be left with 10 cards in each of four suits. If you prefer you could buy Zener cards (available in occult shops), or you can make some yourself.

Simple Telepathy Test

In this simple test the idea is for the Sender to transmit to the Receiver the suit of each card. Since there are four suits you would expect one in every four guesses to be right just by chance. (If you use ESP cards you would expect to get one in every five guesses right by chance.)

Sit on one side of a table, with your friend opposite. Take it in turns to be Sender and Receiver. Shuffle the cards thoroughly and cut them, face down. Place them in a neat pile in front of you, ready to begin.

When both of you are ready, turn up the top card towards you so that you can see it but the Receiver can't, and think about the suit. The Receiver then calls out the suit. If the guess was right put the card, face down, in one pile. If it was wrong put it in a second pile. This way you can easily count how many the Receiver got right.

(If you find you have any trouble remembering which pile is which, or think you might make a mistake, take a large sheet of paper and write 'Right' and 'Wrong' at the top, and put the two piles underneath.)

By chance you should get about ten right. To be sure of getting ten right the Receiver would only have to say 'Hearts' for every single card – since there are ten Hearts in the pack there are bound to be ten correct guesses. You might get 11, 12 or even 13 by chance – if you are lucky. (If you are using ESP cards you can expect to get five out of 25 right by chance).

Figure 1.6: A simple ESP card test.

If you did much better, you must be communicating with your friend, but is it by telepathy? If you got promising results with this simple test you will want to know whether you are really telepathic or not. To find out you need to think up – and then eliminate – all the other possible ways you might have been communicating.

Controls in ESP experiments are important. Sometimes two people seem to communicate by telepathy when in fact they are signalling to each other by tapping on the table, nodding and winking, or otherwise passing secret messages. Or they might unconsciously pick up clues from each other's body language – or the cards might be slightly see-through, or the designs reflected in a window or even a watch face. All of these possibilities have to be ruled out in your experiment before you can claim that you have really observed telepathy.

Controlled Telepathy Experiment

The point of this experiment, like the test above, is to communicate the suits of a sequence of cards from one mind to another.

Apart from yourself, you need two friends, so that you have Experimenter, Sender, and Receiver. The test will find out whether the Sender and Receiver pair can beat chance.

What You Need

- 3 people: Sender, Receiver and Experimenter
- 2 separate rooms for testing
- A pack of ordinary playing cards with the court cards (kings, queens and jacks) removed – or use Zener cards.
- 2 watches or clocks with second hands to co-ordinate timing
- A Sender's Record Sheet (see *pages 20–21*)
- A Receiver's Record Sheet (see pages *20–21)*
- Two pens

Preparations

Before you start the test you need ten minutes to prepare the rooms and the test materials.

Ideally you should use two rooms that are quite separate from each other. Try not to use adjoining rooms, or rooms above each other, just in case one of your friends thinks it would be fun to knock on the ceiling or wall to give the answers away. Two rooms on opposite sides of a hallway would be good.

One room is for the Sender and Experimenter. The other is for the Receiver. Everyone should be sitting comfortably. Ideally the Sender and Experimenter should sit opposite each other across a table. The Experimenter has the cards and shows them to the Sender. The Receiver just needs a comfortable chair and somewhere to write down the guesses. Before you begin, get the rooms ready and put the answer sheets in the right rooms, with a pen each.

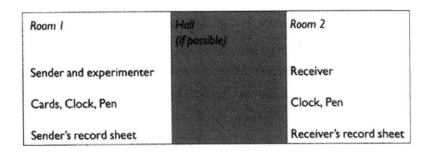

Room I	Hall (if possible)	Room 2
Sender and experimenter		Receiver
Cards, Clock, Pen		Clock, Pen
Sender's record sheet		Receiver's record sheet

Table 1.1 Room layout for ESP experiment.

Decide who is to be Sender, who Receiver, and who Experimenter. If you want to test someone who claims to be psychic, he or she should act as Receiver. If you have friends who think they can communicate by using telepathy, then they may choose who is to send and who is to receive, or you can run the test first one way round and then the other.

Procedure

The procedure may sound quite complicated, but once you have read it through several times you will understand what needs to happen at each stage. Just to make sure everyone knows what he or she has to do, it is well worth doing a few practice trials. Decide to do, for example, five guesses for your practice. Throw these results away. Then you can begin for real.

The Experimenter's Job

Explain to both participants that their task is to try to communicate, by telepathy, the suit of a playing card (or the pattern on a Zener card). In one room the Sender will look at a new card every 15 seconds and try to think about its suit and nothing else. The Receiver will be in another room, trying to guess the suit.

Both should ignore numbers and colours and just think about the card's suit: Spade, Heart, Diamond or Club.

Explain that they are not expected to get every guess right, but that if they have any telepathic power they will get more right than you would expect by chance.

Take the Receiver into the Receiver's room, ensure that he or she is comfortable and then explain what you are going to do. Hand over the record sheet and explain how to fill in the guesses using the following code:

C for Clubs **D** for Diamonds **H** for Hearts **S** for Spades

If you are using Zener cards the Receiver can simply draw the designs from the cards as they appear at the top of his or her record sheet.

Synchronize your watch with the Receiver's watch. This is most important since you need to be sure the Receiver is actually guessing at the same time that the Sender is looking at each card. Decide on a starting time, perhaps about one minute after the time you are going to leave the Receiver, and tell him or her to start then.

The Sender will look at a new card every 15 seconds, that is, four cards a minute. To make sure that your timing does not go astray fill in the times on the Receiver's Record Sheet before you leave – e.g. starting at 7.20, then writing 7.21, 7.22 and so on, leaving space to write four guesses in each minute – we have left spaces for four guesses in each minute on the sheet provided on pages 20–21.

Let the Receiver ask any further questions and make sure he or she is confident about the experiment before you leave. Now check your watches one last time, leave the room and shut the door. If you like you can tape a piece of paper across the gap where the door closes and sign it, so that if the Receiver comes out (for example to try to peek through the door of the Sender's room) the paper will break – and you will be warned that you had a cheat in your test.

Next go into the Sender's room and sit down opposite the Sender. You will stay here for the duration of the guessing. Shuffle the cards thoroughly and place them face down in front of the Sender, saying that you will turn the cards over one by one at 15-second intervals. Fill in the times on the Sender's Sheet as you did for the Receiver. Make sure the Sender understands, and answer any further questions if necessary. Watch the time carefully so that you are ready to begin at the same time as the Receiver begins.

When the pre-arranged time comes, turn over the first card and hold it up away from you, so that the Sender can see it but you cannot. Hold it there for about 10 seconds. Then put it face down on a new pile, and get ready to show the next card when the 15 seconds are up.

The point of not looking yourself is that if you can't see the cards, you can't interfere with any telepathic impressions. However, it does not matter too much if you glimpse a card by mistake.

Continue in this way, making sure that you are sticking to the correct times, until all the cards have been seen.

At this point do not fetch the Receiver. You need to record the order of the cards first. Turn the pack over and write the suit of each card on the Sender's Record Sheet in the order in which the Sender looked at them.

Now you can fetch the Receiver and together you can all check the guesses against the actual cards and find out how many the Receiver got right. The best way is probably for the Sender to call out the suits, one by one, while you write them down on the Receiver's Sheet. Then go through and tick the ones that were right.

ESP EXPERIMENT (Playing cards)   **Sender's Record Sheet**

Sender's Name.. Date.....................................
Receiver's Name... Start Time...........................
Experimenter's Name ....

Time																				
Trial number	1	2	3	4	5	6	7	8	9	10	11	12	13	14	15	16	17	18	19	20
Suit																				

Time																				
Trial number	21	22	23	24	25	26	27	28	29	30	31	32	33	34	35	36	37	38	39	40
Suit																				

ESP EXPERIMENT (Playing cards)   **Receiver's Record Sheet**

Sender's Name.. Date.....................................
Receiver's Name... Start Time...........................
Experimenter's Name ....

Time																				
Trial number	1	2	3	4	5	6	7	8	9	10	11	12	13	14	15	16	17	18	19	20
Suit guessed																				
Correct answer																				
Tick if correct																				

Time																				
Trial number	21	22	23	24	25	26	27	28	29	30	31	32	33	34	35	36	37	38	39	40
Suit guessed																				
Correct answer																				
Tick if correct																				

Total Correct ....

ESP EXPERIMENT (ESP cards) **Sender's Record Sheet**

Sender's Name... Date...................................
Receiver's Name... Start Time...........................
Experimenter's Name ....

Time																
Trial number	1	2	3	4	5	6	7	8	9	10	11	12	13	14	15	16
Symbol																

Time									
Trial number	17	18	19	20	21	22	23	24	25
Symbol									

ESP EXPERIMENT (ESP cards) **Receiver's Record Sheet**

Sender's Name... Date...................................
Receiver's Name... Start Time...........................
Experimenter's Name ....

Time																
Trial number	1	2	3	4	5	6	7	8	9	10	11	12	13	14	15	16
Symbol																
Correct answer																
Tick if correct																

Time									
Trial number	17	18	19	20	21	22	23	24	25
Symbol									
Correct answer									
Tick if correct									

Total Correct ....

Results

By chance alone you would expect to get one in four right, and so the chance score is ten. For example, if you write C for Clubs on every single guess you are bound to be right ten times, since there are ten Clubs in the pack. (If you are using ESP cards you can expect to get one in five right, so the chance score is five out of 25. If you guessed wavy lines every time you would get five right because there are five of each symbol in the pack.)

If you get 11 or 12 right (or six or seven ESP cards) it is still likely to be due to chance, but if you get 20 it is very unlikely that it can be put down to chance alone. This question – of how likely some result is to occur by chance – is the basis for all the statistical tests that scientists do to find out whether their results are 'significant'. You can find out for your experiment by looking up your result in the table below. This will tell you the probability of getting your result by chance.

Significant results in card guessing	
Playing cards (without court cards)	The most likely number of hits is 10
Guessing the correct suit; 40 trials	For a significant result (probability less than 5 per cent) you need to score fewer than 7 or more than 14 hits.
ESP or Zener cards	The most likely number of hits is 5
Guessing the correct symbol; 25 trials	For a significant result (probability less than 5 per cent) you need to score fewer than 2 or more than 8 hits.

Scientists tend to think a result is 'significant' if the probability of its happening is less than 0.05, or 5 per cent. If you get a probability of less than 5 per cent you know your result was unlikely to be just chance, and it might be evidence of telepathy.

Conclusion

How did you do? If your result was just what you expected by chance, you may conclude that your friends are not very telepathic. Of course you cannot conclude that telepathy does not exist – only that on this occasion you did not find evidence of it.

What if you did very badly? You can see from the table above that it is just as unlikely to get very few right as it is to get very many right. So what do you conclude if you do badly? Some parapsychologists argue that getting too few right is just as good evidence of telepathy as getting too many. They call it 'psi-missing'. Possibly your Sender and Receiver can communicate – but used their ability to choose the *wrong* suit.

If your result was well above the odds you may be excited. But was the result really due to telepathy? To be convinced about this you have to be sure that there was *no other way* your Sender and Receiver could have communicated. Did you ensure that they could not see each other, make noises, or send cunning messages?

Most parapsychologists are extremely careful when it comes to concluding that they have really found evidence of telepathy. They would not be happy with this experiment as 'proof', for several reasons.

One argument is that shuffling the cards is not a good enough method of choosing a random order. They would prefer to use random number tables or a computer's random-number generator.

Nevertheless, to score well in a controlled experiment like this would certainly be impressive. Maybe there is a sixth sense after all!

Is ESP Real?

If ESP is real, science has been ignoring its existence for more than 100 years. If it is not real, vast numbers of people have been deluded into believing it is. Which is right?

Were the Sinclairs using 'mental radio'? The pictures we showed looked remarkably similar, but then we deliberately chose those two because they were remarkably alike. In fact Mary Sinclair had drawn *five* little drawings during her and her husband's 'test' (see Figure 1.7).

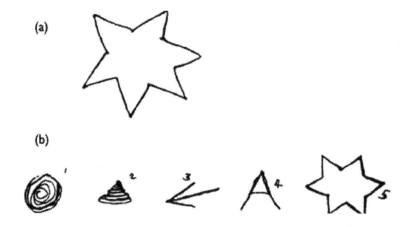

Figure 1.7: Mental Radio revisited: (a) Upton Sinclair's drawing and (b) Mary Craig Sinclair's five drawings. Only the last clearly resembled the target.

If you select only the impressive cases and forget the rest, there will always seem to be telepathy. We don't even know that these five were all she drew. Nor do we know what Mr Sinclair said before they began. He might have said, 'Experiment 16, let's begin,' or 'Let's do some simple little

▶

drawings today. I'm not going to do something very compli- cated, but not just a circle or square either.' In this case she could hardly fail.

You will also now realize that the Sinclair experiments were fatally flawed because Mr Sinclair chose which pictures to draw. He and his wife would have many thoughts in common and, indeed, they might both have been reading the same book about star-gazing that very morning. More recent sci- entific experiments have been far better designed, but the controversy over their results goes on none the less.

2

Crystals

Crystals are beautiful, sometimes even breathtaking. They look precious – and they can be stunningly expensive. They feel wonderfully smooth and hard, and just to hold one is often a great pleasure. Crystals have been around for ages – since long before human beings first walked on the Earth. Indeed, many of the crystals you see today are far older than the human race. Partly because of these qualities, crystals may seem to possess a life or a presence of their own, and many people believe that crystals are capable not only of focusing energy but of bringing about healing and all sorts of other beneficial, spiritual and even magical effects.

Is this true – or just hocus-pocus? All sorts of claims are made for a wide variety of crystals; some simple and some much more elaborate.

Beryl is supposed to strengthen the breathing and circulation systems, not to mention the eyes and the throat. In 1220 Arnoldus Saxo claimed it made his intellect sharper; he wore a bit in battle and said it made him unconquerable, and yet more amiable.

Carnelian is said to be in tune with the resonant energies of the Earth, and to help you feel safe and comfortable. It is supposed to help people who lack the confidence to speak in public, to keep away evil, to improve motivation, and beneficially to affect the genitals. Some say it purifies the liver and blood, and one woman claims that not only does it staunch the flow of blood – she uses it as a cure for a nosebleed – but she wears one in a pouch round her neck to relieve her period pains.

Quartz is supposed to attract the powers of light and energy and so act as a general healer. It is thought to help plants grow better and make cut flowers last longer. People claim that it increases spiritual sensitivity and opens the psychic centres.

Annie is an elderly woman who fell on her garden path and injured her arm; it was painful for a few weeks. Then the bruises subsided and she was able to use her arm normally again – except that she could not lift her hand above her shoulder. This was most inconvenient; she had to brush her hair with the wrong hand and she had considerable difficulty in taking things off high shelves in the kitchen. The doctor she visited was unable to help, but a friend who came to visit her was a healer who worked with crystals. He came twice a week and used a quartz crystal to try to heal the 'aura' in her shoulder. She said she felt the shoulder getting warm during the treatment. After three weeks two large bruises appeared and then faded away, and she found she could use her shoulder normally once more.

You will find masses of detailed information in crystal books, but here is a brief outline of a few of the things that are meant to be improved by some of the more popular crystals:

- *agate* – vitality, self-confidence
- *amethyst* – intuition, serenity
- *adventurine* – tranquillity, anti-migraine

- *beryl* – relieves stress
- *carnelian* – sexual energy
- *citrine* – self-esteem, hope
- *fluorite* – concentration
- *haematite* – courage, optimism
- *jasper* – relieves depression and guilt
- *lapis lazuli* – vitality, creativity
- *moonstone* – helps dieting, friendship
- *obsidian* – eyesight, positivity
- *onyx* – concentration, self-control
- *sodalite* – wisdom, healing
- *tiger's eye* – power, will, insight
- *topaz* – relieves insomnia
- *tourmaline* – encourages sleep, reduces fear
- *turquoise*–strength, peace of mind

Finding a Crystal

You may be lucky enough to live near a rocky beach strewn with beautiful stones. Pebbles on the beach may be composed of a variety of minerals, and are usually polished by the action of the sea. You may have a quarry nearby. Be careful in and near quarries, which are dangerous places; but if you can go there safely you may be fortunate and find crystals lying about. If you have no beach or quarry, you can go to mineral or New Age shops, which usually have a number of crystals for sale.

Choose one you really like. Do not pick a piece of quartz because the book says you should and don't necessarily choose the cheapest – nor the most expensive! If possible, go for the crystal you find most attractive, for then you will enjoy working with it. In a shop with a variety of stones to choose from, some experts say you should close your eyes, think positively and then open them slowly and see whether one of the crystals seems to be glowing brightly. Or perhaps hold your hand over the table and see which crystal feels warmest, or which your hand is attracted to.

There are many books about crystals and they give detailed instructions about how to prepare, revitalize and care for your crystal. For example:

- *Wash it (without detergent) by holding it in your hand in cold running water, preferably in a clear stream – or*
- *Surround it with the smoke from burning sage – or*
- *Imagine it surrounded by a shower of pure white light*
- *Leave it in the direct rays of the sun for an hour or two, to absorb the energy.*
- *Place it under a pyramid to renew its power.*
- *Keep it in a soft leather pouch to guard it from scratches.*

By all means follow these instructions, although a scientist might find it hard to believe that a stone which has been lying around for a million years, possibly on a beach, is going to be much changed by being washed or put in the sun for an hour.

Two Ways to Use Crystals – Passive or Active

To use a crystal passively, put it in a significant place and allow it to influence your life. For example, if you want to do your homework more effectively, you might like to try putting your favourite crystal on your desk or table while you are working. If you want to sleep better or to improve your dreams – or your love life – put it under your pillow when you go to bed. If you would like to increase your concentration and assertiveness at work, place the crystal in a powerful spot at your work station, where you can see it – and it can 'see' you.

I am writing this paragraph with four different crystals balanced on my word processor. Does it make the paragraph any better? I can't tell, but I have had them on my desk all the time I have been writing this book.

To use a crystal actively, you need to interact with it. The simplest way is to carry it around with you, either in a pocket or in a pouch, perhaps hung round your neck; or you can wear it as a piece of jewellery. But first, just hold your crystal. You can feel its power. Hold it snugly in your hand. Allow your warmth to flow into it for at least five minutes, and then gradually feel the 'healing energy' flow back up your arm. What can you feel? You might like to make notes on what the crystal seems to do for you.

Meditation

Meditation with crystals is recommended by several authorities. Apart from the crystal, you need a reasonably peaceful spot, and time on your own – or with someone else who is also meditating.

Soft, warm lighting is good – perhaps a bedside lamp. If you are sitting, place the crystal two or three feet in front of you, on the floor, a cushion or a low table, so that you can look at it easily. If you are lying down, hold the crystal in both hands or place it on your chest or on your forehead.

The position in which you meditate is very important. This need not be because of any mumbo-jumbo about crossed legs or magical forces, but because your physical position affects your mental state. If you lie down there is a danger you will fall asleep, but on the other hand if you are uncomfortable or unstable you may have to keep shifting – and so disturb your meditation. The *ideal position for meditation is one in which you are alert but comfortable.* The traditional 'lotus' position is useful, if you can manage it. The knees and bottom are on the ground, forming a stable triangle, the feet are tucked over the calves, and the back is straight. In this position meditators can stay alert but also relax without falling over.

The problem is, most people can't get into the lotus position without a lot of practice. So the best thing is to try to find a similar one that will do just as well. You could try sitting cross-legged, but it's hard to keep your back straight with your legs crossed. What many experienced meditators do, therefore, is to sit on a hard cushion with both legs tucked in, one alongside the other, in front of it. The cushion is important because it will lift your bottom above your knees and stop your back slumping forwards. Make sure you put both knees on the floor and tuck both feet as far under you as possible, ankles not crossed but one foot against the other ankle. This way you can keep your back nice and straight without any strain.

You might like to make yourself a meditation stool, which is essentially a little angled seat about six inches off the ground, which you can sit on and tuck your feet under with your knees on the ground. You can adopt the same position on a little stool such as a foot-stool.

You can sit in a straight-backed chair, or one of those special kneeling chairs that keep your back upright. Some crystal books recommend lying down – but do this only if you think you can avoid falling straight to sleep.

Play soft meditation music if you find it helps. We prefer to listen to natural sounds – birds, wind, rain, even traffic as long as it is not too loud. You may like to light a joss stick or have some flowers nearby.

Figure 2.1: A good position is most important for meditation. You should be alert but relaxed and comfortable, with your back straight. Looking at a beautiful crystal aids concentration.

Now, having found your position, relax and begin to let your mind calm down. Look at your crystal, or visualize it with your eyes shut – or alternate between these two methods. As the meditation proceeds you might like to imagine a circle of pure white light spiralling out from your crystal and gradually enveloping your whole body.

Try meditating for 10 minutes.

Do not consciously think of anything. The object of meditation is to let thoughts and the self drop away; simply observe stray ideas as they pop into your mind, but do not pursue them. To think of nothing is hard; this is where the crystal positively helps. When your thoughts get distracting, bring your mind gently back to the crystal. Let your eyes rest on it and allow thoughts and sounds and smells around you to flow on their way; just keep looking at the crystal.

Ten minutes may seem a long time for your first meditation, but it will appear to get shorter. If you use a favourite crystal regularly you will probably find that it seems to take on a life of its own. In different lights it looks quite different. As you get more adept at meditation, time seems to slow down. If you place your crystal in sunlight coming through the window, or outside in the garden, you may watch as the shadows gradually move – something we rarely stay still long enough to notice in our ordinary lives.

Many people resent the idea of 'wasting' 10 minutes thinking about 'nothing', but during and after the meditation they feel better – more in tune with themselves and the world, calmer, and more ready to accept life and its trials. See whether this works for you.

Meditation certainly works for a great many people. For thousands of years people have practised various ways of calming their minds. In this way they have found peace and mental freedom. Some people have achieved states in which they feel at one with the universe; others have found insight into the nature of mind and its relationship to the world. But this takes much practice and real dedication; it is a slow process to re-educate the mind – to change it from a chaotic mess to a calm and open space.

Many of us spend hours and hours worrying about awful things that might happen in the future. We agonize about what other people think of us. We hate our own bodies, and think we are too fat, too spotty, too slow or too incompetent. Or we get maddened that other people seem to be favoured all the time. Most of these fears and dreads are of imaginary futures, and we would be better off without them. Meditation can help. Effective meditators, who can calm the mind and allow the self to fall away, cease to worry about these imaginary futures. They learn to live in the present moment and

33

accept things as they are. This is not easy, but it does help you through life.

The question that arises is 'Does the crystal make any difference?' Can you side-step all that long practice just by having the right crystal next to you when you meditate? Or is the crystal just acting as a helpful focus to stop your mind wandering? If the crystal is only a point of focus, then any small object ought to do just as well. Try it and see. Is your meditation any different with and without the crystal?

The trouble with this is that you can see whether the crystal is there or not. To find out objectively whether crystals have magical powers you would need to do some properly controlled experiments.

How Could Crystals Work?

If you believe all the claims that are made for crystals then you must accept that they have special powers of various kinds – powers at present not endorsed by science or understood in any ordinary scientific theory – powers such as focusing earth energies, resonating with people's personal frequencies, attracting occult powers and producing healing rays.

Be wary of the claims you read. Many of them are mistaken, for they are frequently based on scientific errors. For example, quartz is made of silica, or silicon dioxide, and is chemically the same stuff as sand; so there is plenty of it on Earth. Quartz crystals have been used in radios, and they are used as oscillators in many precision watches and clocks. But quartz is *not* the main constituent of electronic chips or integrated circuits (as has been claimed). Nor do quartz crystals provide the *power* for our watches or radios. They are inert lumps of stone. It therefore seems most unlikely that crystals can have a direct effect on our minds.

Sceptics claim that all the powers are really in your own mind. For example, you may be able to 'feel' your crystal's energy, but sceptics would argue that you merely imagine that 'healing energy' is flowing back from the crystal. Imagery can be very powerful. If you imagine you can do something it may give you the extra confidence you need. If you imagine your favourite food you might even find your mouth watering.

You may feel that your meditation is better when you have your crystal near you, but again cynics would argue that the crystal only helps meditation by acting as a focus point, or helping you to believe you can meditate, rather than by exerting any magical influence. The greatest value of a crystal may well be as an aid in meditation. Crystals are beautiful; they can fill us with delight and take our minds away from the hurtful feelings that might otherwise fill them. The main difficulty in meditation is that you get distracted by intrusive thoughts. Looking at a crystal may help you to avoid those distractions. Focus on the crystal, and forget your self.

So we now have two completely opposed theories. One theory is that crystals have magical powers. If this is so, science is ignoring something that could change our lives and our understanding of the world.

The other theory is that crystals themselves have no power at all – instead all their supposed effects come from people's own minds. If this is true, the crystal-sellers are making unfair claims about what their crystals can do – as well as lots of money. But which is true? The only way to find out is to do some properly designed experiments.

A Simple Experiment

When you held your crystal did you feel its energy? Did a tingling seem to flow down your arm? How long does it flow back? Is there a difference between how it feels when you hold it in your right hand and your left? Do different crystals behave in different ways?

You might like to do a whole sequence of tests to try and find the answers to these questions. Will the stone still work if you don't actually touch it? Put the crystal in a plastic bag and see whether you can still feel its 'power'. Write the answers down as you get them; otherwise you may well forget later what you noticed at the time.

If a bag is no barrier, try a tougher test; put your crystal in a cardboard box and see whether you can feel the power through the cardboard. For a direct comparison, put an ordinary rock in a second identical box. Can you feel the difference?

If this test is successful (that is, the box containing the crystal feels different), you might think this proves that the crystal has power. But this is not a good test – the main reason being that you put the crystal there yourself. You knew which box contained the crystal and which the ordinary rock – and that is all your imagination needs to get to work. So you need a better experiment. Here are some ideas for more scientific experiments.

Experiment 1

Can you feel the warmth radiating from any of your crystals? Can you 'see' the energy they put out? If so, you can test whether these effects are all in your mind or actually coming from the crystal itself.

To run these tests you really need a friend to mix up the specimens so that you don't know which is which. If you try to do it yourself you are likely to fool yourself – and the tests will no longer be rigorous or meaningful.

Take your favourite crystal, and two ordinary pebbles or stones, each of about the same size and weight as the crystal.

Take some newspaper or a tissue to wrap each stone in. Find three similar small containers which you cannot see through. You could use small cardboard boxes such as individual cereal packets, yogurt pots with lids, dark plastic bags – or even socks, which you can wrap thoroughly around the stones and fasten with sticky tape or rubber bands. Label the containers A, B, and C.

> *Step 1.* Put the three stones (the crystal and two ordinary stones) loosely into their tissue or paper and then into the containers – but for now leave them open so that you can see in. Now try to 'feel' the power of the crystal as you have done before. If you can still feel the warmth or energy you can be sure that the containers are not going to block any effect of the crystal.

> Step 2. Now you need to find out whether you can still 'feel' the power when you don't know where the crystal is.

Ask your friend, while you are out of the room and not looking, to wrap each stone and place it in one of the containers, and fasten them all up. When you come back into the room the stones should all be invisible and you must not be able to see or feel by weight or shape which container has your crystal in it.

Place the three containers on the table in front of you. Touch them, one by one, with your fingers. Can you feel the warmth or the 'energy' flowing out of your crystal? If so, which container has your crystal inside?

Once you have decided and written down your choice – A, B or C – you could open the container and see whether you are right. But the experiment isn't foolproof yet.

You could get the correct container just by chance – you have one chance in three of being lucky. There are two possible ways to make more certain.

Method A:

Do the experiment five times running. Mix up the containers and feel them again. The trouble is you are bound to recognize which is the container you have already chosen, and if you believe your first choice was right you will probably go on choosing the same one.

One solution is to ask your friend to mix them up each time you have chosen, and then give them to you under a sheet of paper. You have to choose, without looking or touching, just by the warmth coming through the paper.

Method B:

Involve other people in the tests. If possible, ask five (or even 10) people separately to write down which of the three containers they can feel warmth coming from. They must all write down their answers separately and secretly before anyone reveals what he or she thinks.

For either method you can use the Crystals Record Sheet (see *page* 39) to record your results. If you have properly concealed the stones, then you can find out whether your result was likely to be just chance. If you are right four times out of five, or at least seven times out of 10, then you can be fairly certain (more than 95 per cent) that your result was real; not just luck.

You may think that 10 trials is too many. Decide in advance whether you are going to do five or 10. There is a record sheet for each. *You must not leave any results out.* The statistics will not be meaningful if, for example, you fail to write down one test which got a poor result. If you have done everything properly and if you get at least four out of five trials right, or seven out of 10, then your crystals are really working.

Record Sheet for Crystal Experiments (Five trials)

Trial	Guess; is crystal A, B, or C?	Correct answer (A, B, or C)	Tick if correct
1			
2			
3			
4			
5			

Total Correct ....

If you get four or five right out of five, your result is significant.

Record Sheet for Crystal Experiments (Ten trials)

Trial	Guess; is crystal A, B, or C?	Correct answer (A, B, or C)	Tick if correct
1			
2			
3			
4			
5			
6			
7			
8			
9			
10			

Total Correct ....

If you get seven or more right, your result is significant.

Experiment 2

This is a passive experiment, designed to find out whether your crystal can influence its surroundings directly. In this case, can a crystal make cut flowers last longer? (The idea was suggested by a helpful section in Ursula Markham's book *Discover Crystals* [Aquarian, 1988].)

Buy or pick a bunch of flowers. Any flowers will do; they don't need to be expensive. Even daisies from the lawn are all right as long as they look fresh when you pick them. Divide your bunch into three equal groups, and put each group into a similar vase or glass (or yogurt carton or egg-cup) of water.

Place containers A, B and C close to the three vases – inside them if possible, or underneath, or close beside them. If you use black plastic bags (such as a bit cut off a dustbin liner) you can put the stones right inside the vases – but make sure you cannot possibly tell which is which by looking at them.

Figure 2.2: A simple experiment with cut flowers. Does a quartz crystal help them last longer? The other two parcels contain another crystal and an ordinary garden stone. Can you tell which is which from the state of the flowers?

Leave all the flowers to stand side by side on the same windowsill or table for two or three days. Try to make sure they all get the same amount of light from the window, and that none is standing over a radiator or other source of direct heat. You may notice that one vase is in a better position than the others. Do your best to make them all equally well off. You may think it fairer if you move the vases around each day to give them all a chance of the best position. As long as you do not know which contains the crystal, it does not matter exactly how you try to ensure equal conditions for them all.

After two days, note how well the flowers have lasted: Have any heads died completely? Do they all look tired and brown? You need to work out your own way of judging which bunch is doing the best. You might like to count the number of heads still in good shape – or of dead flowers in each vase. In any case, *write down which bunches you reckon have lasted the best and the worst*

Repeat the process on days three and four, and when the flowers are obviously beginning to die decide which vase you think has had the benefit of the crystal. Look at the letter on the container and *write your answer down.* Then open up the wrapping and see whether you were right. One book we read claimed that flowers would last about two days longer than normal. This ought to be easy enough to detect.

Did you manage to detect the crystal by its effect on the flowers? As before, one success could just be luck. So, if possible, repeat the experiment, using the Record Sheet provided (see page 38). If you pick the right container four out of five times, you know your success is unlikely to be just down to chance.

When you actually try this experiment you will find it takes quite a long time and uses quite a lot of flowers, since to get a significant result you must do it five times, and each test takes three bunches and four or five days; so that means 15 bunches of flowers and about three or four weeks in all. So we recommend using small bunches of cheap flowers – say two or three daisies – in yogurt pots or egg-cups, and a table or shelf or windowsill that, even when it seems always to be covered with dying flowers, no one else is going to complain about – or even worse, decide to 'clear up', throwing the flowers away.

What conclusions can you draw from your experiments? Can a crystal really make flowers last longer? Or is it just a gimmicky claim put about by the people who want to sell crystals? With real experimental results you can make up your own mind.

You might also like to devise your own tests to find out whether crystals have any effect on the growth of pot plants, or the germination of seeds.

Crystals and Dreams

Some people say crystals have an amazing effect on their sleep. They say that with a crystal under the pillow they sleep better, and wake more refreshed – and that their dreams are more enjoyable and pleasant. If this were true for everyone it would be good news indeed. Insomnia, broken sleep and nightmares are common problems, and many people go to doctors and psychiatrists because they cannot sleep properly.

Enormous quantities of sleeping pills are consumed every year, but they often have noxious side-effects and frequently create addiction. If simply placing a crystal under the pillow could help people to sleep, we could solve all these problems at a stroke.

But is it true? Can a crystal really affect sleep and dreams? There is only one way to find out: Do some experiments.

First of all you will need to keep a record of your sleeping patterns. Put a notebook by your bed. Each morning write down how well you slept, and for how long. You might like to do this for a week, and then put a crystal under your pillow. Record your sleep for another week and see whether there has been any change.

Did you seem to sleep better? If you did, can you now conclude that the crystal affected your sleep?

The problem here is that you knew there was a crystal under your pillow and you knew that it was supposed to help you sleep. You might have slept better because you had more confidence in falling asleep. Or you might have kidded yourself that you slept better even when you didn't, just because you expected – or wanted – the crystal to work. The only way to do a proper experiment is to make sure you don't know whether or not you have a real crystal under your pillow.

As before, you will need a friend to help you by preparing three containers – a sensible way to do this is to take three different socks (say red, blue, and stripy) and ask your friend to wrap the crystal in one and ordinary stones in the other two, rolling all three up in a similar way. *You must not peek, or find out which stone is where.*

Keep the three rolled-up socks by your bed. Each night, for three nights, pick one to put under your pillow. Record which sock you used each night. In the morning record your sleep patterns. Then, on the basis of this record, decide which night you had the best sleep. Write down which sock you think has the crystal in.

If you decide to do this five times (that is, for 15 nights) or 10 times (30 nights), you can use the Record Sheets on page 39. Once again, you need to get four out of five right – or seven out of 10 – to know your result is unlikely to have been just a fluke.

Exploring the effect of crystals on dreams is a little harder, but in the next chapter we explain how to keep a dream diary.

What can you now conclude? Do crystals really have a magical effect if you place one under your pillow at night? Would you recommend that your friends buy one?

Can Crystals Affect Us Directly?

The placebo effect is well known in medical science. Experiments show that people can often be made a little better by being given a fake pill or a pretend injection, known as a placebo. A pill made of chalk may not work biochemically in the same way as an aspirin, but if the sufferer *believes* it is aspirin it may be just as effective in easing his or her headache.

Researchers have found that a fake pill given by a senior doctor will have a stronger effect than one given by a young student nurse, and that the colour is important – green placebos are more effective than pink ones in some treatments. Belief can work wonders. So if you believe in the power of crystals you may find they do have a beneficial effect.

If having a crystal makes you feel good, then have a crystal; it is a simple way of improving your outlook on life. But it may well work entirely through your self-perception. This doesn't matter – feeling good is a perfectly acceptable goal – just as long as you do not leap to false conclusions about non-existent powers, rays and energies, or stay away from the doctor when you really need treatment.

Can crystals make cut flowers last longer? We did the experiment described on pages 38–40, using bunches of nasturtiums on the kitchen windowsill. We were intrigued to

▶

---

find that the brownish flowers died faster than the orange or yellow ones, but we failed to find the crystal consistently by noting which bunch lasted longest; in fact we got it wrong twice in three tests.

Of course crystals can do you no harm. The only problem arises when people persuade you to part with your money for a crystal that may not do all that they claim. But if you have done your own experiments you should be able to make your mind up about which claims to believe and which to doubt.

3

Dreams

Everyone dreams. You may not remember your dreams every morning, or even very often, but psychologists are convinced that everyone does dream. If you were taken into a laboratory and wired up to a machine to measure your brain waves, it would be able to record when you were entering REM (Rapid Eye Movement) sleep. You would have a recognizable pattern of brain waves and your eyes would be moving rapidly back and forth as though you were watching something. At that time, if someone were to call your name or shake you awake, you would almost certainly report that you had been dreaming.

Experiments with people sleeping in the laboratory have shown that most people have their first dreaming period after about two hours of sleep. This may last about half an hour, then there is a cycle of dreaming and non-dreaming sleep through the night, with roughly four or five dream-periods in a typical eight-hour sleep. This dreaming sleep must be important for our brains, because it is this kind of sleep that we catch up on first if ever we are deprived of sleep for some reason.

Dreams are often bizarre and strange. The same logic does not apply as in ordinary daily life. You may meet someone who is half your sister and half that woman you met in the supermarket yesterday. You may find yourself trying to reach a hamburger stand in the desert, when your waking self would reject this as absurd, or be running after your cat who had gone off to the park with next door's hamster.

The oddest thing is that we do not seem to be sufficiently aware, in dreams, to realize the incongruity. If we did we might think – 'Wow, this is weird, it must be a dream.' Some people can do this, and this is called 'lucid dreaming', but for most of us the oddities of dream logic carry on quite unchallenged by our conscious minds.

Perhaps because of this strange logic, dreams have often been thought to have a psychic element. Ideas and images can be so odd that they seem to come from somewhere else – not from our own, supposedly rational, minds. There are many civilizations in which dreams are used to try to find out about the future or to enable the dreamer to use extraordinary powers – such as the ability to see over great distances. In many cultures people believe there is a separate dream world – or dream time – and that when you sleep some part of you travels to that other sphere.

Modern psychologists, by contrast, believe that all the material of our dreams comes from the workings of our own brains. They say there is no need to invent another world, or another time to travel in. They reject the idea that we can really see what is happening at a distance during a dream – or that we can communicate with someone else through the power of our dreams.

However, there are many stories that seem to suggest that people can do all of these, in dreams.

An Attack of the Fever

On 11 March 1871 Mrs Morris Griffith had a disturbing dream which she later described in a letter to the Society for Psychical Research:

I awoke in much alarm, having seen my eldest son, then at St Paul de Loanda on the southwest coast of Africa, looking dreadfully ill and emaciated, and I heard his voice distinctly calling to me. I was so disturbed I could not sleep again, but every time I closed my eyes the appearance recurred, and his voice sounded distinctly, calling me 'Mamma.' I felt greatly depressed all through the next day, which was Sunday, but I did not mention it to my husband, as he was an invalid, and I feared to disturb him.

The next day a letter arrived containing some photos of my son, saying he had had a fever but was better, and hoped immediately to leave for a much more healthy station, and written in good spirits.

We heard no more news until the 9th of May, when a letter arrived with the news of our son's death from a fresh attack of fever, on the night of the 11th of March, and adding that just before his death he kept calling repeatedly to me. I did not at first connect the date of my son's death with that of the dream until reminded of it by friends, and also an old servant, to whom I had told it at the time ...

Almost 100 years later Mrs Eileen Garrett wrote of a disturbing dream about her daughter, who was away at boarding school. She had gone to bed worrying about the girl, but then realized that it was Sunday night and so her daughter would at that moment be writing her usual weekly letter home. Mrs Garrett assumed she had 'caught' her daughter's thoughts by telepathy.

I awoke, however, at 2 o'clock in the morning with the impression that she was in the house, and had just been at my side talking to me. In the dream she had said, 'I have not written to you, dear, as my chest hurt. Tonight I am coughing, and have a fever. When the principal found I hadn't written, she was very cross, and called me neglectful and undutiful; but now she has been in my room, and understands that I am not well.'

Although I was still uncertain of the validity of this communication, I decided to write down what she had said. The next morning I again felt disturbed, since no letter had arrived. Remembering my dream, I tele-graphed the head-mistress to inquire if all was well. In her reply she stated that my daughter was in bed with a heavy chest cold, and then continued, half-apolo-getically, to blame what she termed the child's 'sullen behaviour', in refusing to write to me, on the illness.

A subsequent letter from my daughter suggested that she had felt confused, 'not well, hurt, and misun-derstood in the evening'. These were the 'feelings' I had 'caught' in the waking state, before retiring, while the ensuing dream had revealed the illness and the cause of her emotional disturbance, at a time when we were both sleeping ...

Dreams in Ancient Rome

Seemingly paranormal dreams are mentioned in the Bible, and the great Roman orator Marcus Tullius Cicero had at least one himself. He told Caesar and his colleagues about it the next morning, as they were on their way to the Capitol in Rome.

He had seen a noble-looking youth, let down on a chain of gold from the skies, standing at the door of the temple.

At that moment he saw a young man waiting for them. Although he had never met the youth before, Cicero recognized him instantly:

'But there is the actual boy I dreamed of!'

The young man turned out to be Caesar's great-nephew, Octavius, who later took the name Augustus and went on to be Emperor after Caesar's death.

In spite of this remarkable hit, Cicero himself was most sceptical about dreams, and argued strongly that they had no meaning, and that people who claimed to be able to tell the future from dreams were fooling themselves:

Nothing can be imagined so preposterous, so incredible, or so monstrous, as to be beyond our power of dreaming ... those very persons who experience these dreams cannot by any means understand them, and those persons who pretend to interpret them do so by conjecture, not by demonstration ...

And he asked three critical questions:

1. By what method can this infinite variety [of dreams] be either fixed in memory or analysed by reason?
2. Can dreams be experimented on?
3. And if so, how?

This is where you come in. There are ways in which you can try to answer Cicero's critical questions, and that is what the rest of this chapter is all about.

Keeping a Dream Diary

The best way to start investigating your dreams is to keep a dream diary. All you need are a notebook (it need not be elaborate or expensive; a school exercise book is fine) and pen or pencil by your bed, and time to write when you wake up.

Set your alarm to go off 10 minutes earlier than usual, and *as soon as you wake up* write down the story – and all the details – of any dream you can remember. Some people find it difficult to recall their dreams, but if you remember nothing or just a vague feeling, still write that down. If you determinedly make the time to write, you will usually be able to remember something, and once you get into practice you should find recall easier and easier.

The dream diary is the simplest way to begin to answer Cicero's first question – *By what method can dreams be either fixed in memory or analysed by reason?* Memory is notoriously tricky – we all make mistakes in remembering things. And dreams are even harder to remember because they don't make a lot of sense and are not obviously connected to what is going on around us. That is why writing them down at the first opportunity is so important. Once they are written down, and so 'fixed', you can begin to analyse them.

Preferably keep your dream diary going for at least a month; then you will be able to get some idea of how often you can recall dreams, and whether for example you have them more often on some nights of the week than others.

Once you have begun this sort of analysis, you are ready to tackle Cicero's second and third questions: Can dreams be experimented on? And if so, how?

Simple Experiments with Dreams

Some people say bad dreams are caused by indigestion, because if you eat something rich and heavy late at night your stomach has trouble coping with all the food, which affects your general sense of well-being. Why not try it out?

Cheese in particular is said to be bad news. This may be more than an 'old wives' tale', since some chemicals that are hard for some people to digest exist in large quantities in cheese. So try eating a piece of cheese late at night, say on every third day for two or three weeks. At the end of this time, look carefully at your dream diary. Do you have more dreams after cheese – or worse ones – than on cheese-free nights? Does the type of cheese make any difference?

Can you choose your dreams? Some people can decide in advance what they want to dream about, and actually succeed. This is not a common skill, but it can be learned. One method is called 'dream incubation'. The basic idea is to think very hard about whatever it is you want to dream about throughout the day, and especially last thing before going to sleep. You may find that eventually the ideas you have been 'incubating' will pop up in your dreams.

You may find that with practice you can change your dreams halfway through. Wake yourself up in the middle of the night, or take the opportunity when you wake from a dream. Try not to wake up too much, just keep yourself a little dozy. Then go over in your mind what the dream was about, immerse yourself in the feelings and atmosphere of the dream but imagine it going in the direction you desire. As you fall asleep again you may be able to go back into the dream and shape it the way you want.

Do you ever know *at the time* that you are dreaming? This is called 'lucid dreaming' and is another skill that can be learned, though it takes some time and perseverance. One method is to practise when you are awake. With a marker pen write a large D (for Dreaming) on the back of your hand. Every time you notice this 'D', ask yourself 'Am I dreaming or am I awake?' This will get you into the habit of questioning your state of mind. If you do this often enough you should find that sooner or later you do the same thing in your dreams. Sometimes you will then (stupidly!) answer 'I'm awake,' but sometimes you may notice something truly weird or bizarre and conclude that you can only be dreaming. Then you are there – in a lucid dream!

The fun of lucid dreaming is that once you have become aware that it is a dream you can more easily take control of it. 'Right. If this is a dream, that tiger cannot possibly harm me. I shall jump on its back and go for a ride. I shall turn it into my favourite cat and stroke it. I shall...' the possibilities are endless.

One thing that's really fun, if you realize you are dreaming, is to fly. Lots of people have flying dreams, and usually they are most enjoyable. They can be even more fun when you realize fully that it is a dream and that you can do whatever you like. You can swoop above the clouds, dive-bomb your friend's house, or go and visit a country you have never seen before. But... are you really visiting these places, or are they just images conjured up by your own mind from what you know and can imagine?

This takes us to the really interesting question about dreams – their origin.

Where Do the Images Come From?

The images we see in dreams are substantial and often as 'real' to us as what we see when we are awake. Some people don't notice colour in their dreams; others hear no sounds. But the stories in dreams can be intensely dramatic, as can the feelings they provoke. As we get older our dreams get more and more complex and full of detail.

Generally, young children up to the age of about five or six have rather simple and static dreams. They dream of situations or places – but nothing much happens. Sometimes they may wake up screaming from night-terrors or nightmares, but these too are often composed of a nameless dread or indescribable terror, rather than the complicated events adults dream about. As they get older the action in their dreams becomes more and more detailed, reflecting the increase in their powers of imagination and their knowledge of the world. Emotions, too, become gradually more subtle and complex. By the time we are teenagers dreams can be extremely complicated and amusing – or terrifying.

You might wonder why we don't actually run away from the dream monster – or at least kick off the bedclothes in trying to escape. The reason is that during REM sleep the body's muscles are paralysed. This means you can think about almost anything without actually acting it out. That is, unless you go sleep-walking! Interestingly, sleep-walking and sleep-talking happen not in dreaming (REM) sleep, but in ordinary sleep. It is as though by mistake a dream occurs in ordinary sleep, and because the body is not properly paralysed you start to act it out – not a very safe thing to do! But don't worry. Most people wake up if they get into really dangerous situations while sleep-walking. Another 'mistake' can happen when you wake up while your body is still paralysed. This is called 'sleep paralysis' and can be frightening, but it wears off quickly, especially if you just relax and do not fight against it.

Blind people also dream, but their dreams are not visual like those of people who can see. They experience stories just as convoluted, and happenings just as weird, but the dreams consist more of sounds, conversations, touches, and ideas than of pictures.

Why Do We Need to Dream So Much?

Nearly 100 years ago Freud proposed that dreams were wish-fulfilling – that because people were often prevented from carrying out their wishes for real, they did so in their dreams. You might like to look at your own dream diary and try to decide whether or not this theory fits your dreams. Many dreams are so horrible that they could not possibly be anyone's wish – which seems to make the theory unlikely.

Freud might then have argued that the dreams were disguised, but is this a good argument? One severe problem with this Freudian theory is that you can 'explain' almost any dream this way, but when you have done so you really don't understand the origin of dreams any better.

One more recent theory is that dreaming is a good way to practise the kinds of skills we can never practise for real – such as running away from wild beasts (our ancestors might have been eaten if they hadn't practised in their sleep first), facing difficult social situations (we might not dare ask that man to dance if we hadn't practised it beforehand) or trying out possible consequences of our actions (dreaming that we give up our job might help us to decide whether to do so or not).

Another theory is that dreaming is the brain's way of organizing its memory banks. If you see the brain as a digital computer, then perhaps the memory banks get filled up during the day. This could cause malfunctions, and so in dreaming the computer can be taken 'off line' while the information is reorganized and stored more efficiently. However, our brains are not really much like digital computers. For example, the things computers are good at – such as quick calculations – many of us are very bad at. And the things we are best at – such as recognizing people or learning to speak – computers are not easily programmed to do.

A more modern approach uses the idea of 'neural nets'. These are complicated groups of nerve cells that work together to learn associations between things and events. Each network can remember lots of things simultaneously, but the more it stores the more the different things get mixed up, and this could lead to terrible confusion and even to hallucinations. The theory is that in dreaming, the networks are flooded with nerve impulses so that all the weaker memories are flushed out, leaving only the stronger ones to carry on to the next day. The cleaned-up network can then keep on learning. In this theory the function of dreaming is to get rid of unwanted memories – in other words we dream to *forget.* The things in our dreams are just the rubbish our brains are throwing away.

How does it all end up as a convincing dream-story, then? Perhaps this is a demonstration of the fertility of the brain in putting images together to make stories. Even if you dream of something 'impossible' – one moment you are running through a supermarket in your pyjamas, the next you are sharing a swimming pool with a talking shark – each basic image (the supermarket, the pyjamas, the pool, etc.) can have come from your memory – from what you know. The imaginative brain then connects the separate images to make a story that includes them all.

One very appealing idea is that the dream stories are concocted by the brain in an instant, and do not really take up all the time they seem to. French psychologist Alfred Maury reported having a long complicated dream about the French Revolution which ended, abruptly, with his being guillotined! He woke to find that the bed-post had collapsed and was lying on his neck. He wondered whether the falling of the bed-post might have triggered off the whole dream, in which case it must all have happened within a fraction of a second, since the shock of the impact must have wakened him quickly.

However, recent REM studies have shown that most dreams happen in more-or-less real time; so we must assume that Maury's dream had been going on for some time before the bed-post collapsed.

Even if Maury's dream wasn't all made up in an instant it still seems as though the weight on his neck somehow got into his dreams. Maybe you will find this happens in your own dreams. We can certainly take in sounds while we sleep, at least to a limited extent. When the alarm clock rings we often incorporate that sound into our dream – it becomes the bell of the fire engine, or the alarm bells in the sinking ship. Experiments on people dreaming in the laboratory have shown that dripping water on their face can lead to dreams of swimming, or bathing under waterfalls; puffing air on to their hands can make them dream of winds and storms.

If we can absorb *sounds* while dreaming, can we also absorb *pictures?* Since most people sleep in the dark with their eyes shut, this seems impossible. If images could enter the brain under these conditions they would have to do so by some paranormal process such as telepathy. This would be hard to reconcile with what most scientists believe about the way the brain works. So can it happen? You can try to find out for yourself with some simple experiments.

Does Dream Telepathy Work?
Once you have your dream diary going, you are in a strong position to test yourself for dream telepathy. The question is: Can the images in your dreams come from outside?

Ask a friend what he dreamed of last night. Did you find that you both dreamed of similar things? It is easy to find images or ideas in common and, in your enthusiasm, to become convinced that you must have been dreaming the same thing at the same time. But is this evidence of dream telepathy? If you try to think up all the reasons why it may not be, you will be in a good position to devise a better test.

One problem is that most people have fantastically complicated dreams with lots and lots of little details in them. Once you start trying to remember them, more and more details may come back to you, increasing the chance of finding something, however small, that you both dreamed of. Another problem is that you know each other. You may think alike or have friends and experiences in common. It could be these, and not telepathy, that made you dream alike.

You need a better test. For example, if a friend was looking at a picture and thinking about it during the night, could you pick up the impressions from her?

Here is a simple test to find out. On a particular night, get a friend – we'll call her Lucy – to be Sender. She should cut out six striking and very different images from a magazine, number them 1–6, stick them on a card or cards, and put them by her bed. (If you can persuade two or three friends to do this, so much the better.)

At about the time you are going to sleep, Lucy should pick one of the images randomly by throwing a die (for example, if she throws a 4, she should pick image No 4). Then she should hold this image up, stare at it, and think about it for at least five minutes. She should think about all sorts of stories built around this image. She must concentrate hard and go to sleep thinking about the picture.

In the morning, write your dream diary as usual.

You must not communicate with the Sender in any way – nor see *any of the images – until you have written your diary.*

When you have written your diary, ask your friend to give you all six pictures – but do not speak to her. Look at them carefully and try to decide whether any one of them might have been in your dream, or at least have influenced it. For example, if one of the images is of a wolf, and you dreamt about a frightening savage dog, then it is reasonable to guess there might be a connection.

Write down which image you think Lucy was concentrating on and why – mention what you have written in your dream diary which seems to correspond.

Now, for the first time, ask Lucy which image she was concentrating on.

There is one chance in six you will choose the correct image just by guesswork. So getting it right once does not prove you are psychic. However, you would be unlikely to get the correct image twice in a row. The odds against that happening are 35–1 ; it's only a 3 per cent chance.

A More Rigorous Experiment

There are some shortcomings to the experiment just described. Nevertheless, the basic idea is quite sound and parapsychologists have used similar methods to try to detect dream telepathy. Can you think what might be wrong with the simple experiment – so that you can improve it?

One problem is that Lucy might have held tight on to the one picture she chose and left fingerprints on it, crumpled it up a bit, or in some other way made it possible for you to identify it as the target. One solution to this is to use duplicate copies of all the pictures, so that the Sender never touches the ones the Receiver has to choose from.

Another problem is that the experiment relied on you and Lucy being scrupulously honest about not communicating. A more rigorous approach is to have a separate Experimenter whose job it is to make sure that no one cheats.

We suggested that Lucy looked at the picture for five minutes before going to sleep, but maybe it would work better if she were looking at it when the Receiver was actually dreaming. Without a dream laboratory this is impossible to ensure – but we can get a bit closer to the ideal.

You might think of other problems – and try to solve them in a better experiment. Here is our suggestion for a dream telepathy experiment that is well-controlled but can be done at home.

What You Need

- 3 people – Experimenter, Sender, Receiver
- Alarm clock
- 2 copies of each of 6 pictures
- 7 envelopes
- Die (to choose a random number from 1 to 6)
- Notebook and pen to record dreams

Procedure

First decide on who is to take which role in the experiment.

The *Experimenter's* job is to organize things; first, to prepare the pictures in advance.

To make the two sets of six pictures, we suggest you get hold of two copies of the same magazine, and cut six pictures from one of them. Make sure they are all very different. Do not pick six pop stars; rather look for three colour pictures, three black-and-white. Try and find a wide landscape, a building, a face, an animal, a cartoon – or some such group where subject and style vary from one to another.

Lay the pictures out side by side, and write a number (1–6) on each. If you like, stick each of them on a piece of paper or card, and write the number on the card, so that the picture is not too floppy and the writing doesn't show through from the back. Then cut the same pictures from the other copy of the magazine, stick them on paper if you wish and number them, so that the two sets have identical numbers.

Put the Receiver's set – all six pictures – in one (thick) envelope so that they cannot be seen from outside. Seal it sign your name over the edge of the flap, and write RECEIVER'S PICTURES on the outside.

Write on the outsides of the other envelopes SENDER 1, SENDER 2, and so on up to SENDER 6. Put the six pictures in the corresponding envelopes – picture 1 in SENDER 1, and so on. Seal them all up and sign them over the edges of the flaps.

Now you are ready to begin.

During the experiment you have to make sure that the Sender and Receiver cannot communicate with each other (except by telepathy!). Ideally you should sleep in the same house as either the Sender or the Receiver. In this way you can make sure they do not get in touch during the night. The other person can be in the next room, in a neighbouring house, or miles away – it does not matter. Indeed, it might be interesting to try the experiment with people who are very far apart from one another.

Decide on a night for your first test. Give the Receiver the notebook and pen, and tell him carefully what to do. Give the Sender the six SENDER envelopes and the die, and tell her what to do. Make sure you leave the room before she begins, so that you don't know what number she throws nor what the target picture is.

The *Receiver's* job is to go to bed and switch off the light at a time you specify, for example 11 p.m. (you can choose any time, as long as you all agree to it). *As soon as he wakes up* he must write down a detailed report of all the dreams he remembers. This applies particularly in the morning, but encourage him to write a dream report if he wakes in the middle of the night.

The *Sender's* job is first to set her alarm for 6 a.m. Then, at 10.55 p.m. (or 5 minutes before the Receiver is to go to bed), she has to throw the die once, and open the indicated envelope – e.g. if she throws a 5, open envelope 5, for Picture 5 is the target. *She must not open any of the other envelopes.* Then, before falling asleep she should look carefully at the target picture for at least 10 minutes. She should concentrate on it; imagine the scenes it shows as clearly as possible; think about any associations and links and stories connected with the picture; and in general get as much immersed as possible in whatever the picture shows.

Then she should lay the picture face down, perhaps under her pillow, and switch off the light. If she stays awake for a bit, or wakes in the middle of the night, she should keep thinking about the target picture. The picture should be out of sight in case someone tries to sneak a look at it in the night. When the alarm goes at 6 a.m., she should pick up the target picture and concentrate on it again. This should be before the Receiver wakes up, and is a good time for dreaming. At 6.15 she can hide the picture again and go back to sleep. When she finally wakes, she must keep the picture and all the envelopes hidden until she hears from the Experimenter.

Later in the day the *Experimenter* should meet the Receiver and give him the sealed envelope of RECEIVER'S PICTURES. If your Receiver is far away you can send the pictures by post; do this in advance if you like, as long as the Receiver does not open them before completing the dream report.

The *Receiver* must then sit down in a quiet place, go through everything he has written in his dream report, and then open the envelope and compare his dreams with each picture. Then he should rank all the pictures – that is, put them in order from the closest match to the furthest away – and write the order down on the report, with reasons. For example '1st choice Pic 4 (tennis racket) because I dreamed of hitting something with a frying pan. 2nd choice tree, because my dream was green and shimmery ...'

When this is done the Receiver should let the Experimenter know. At this point – but not before – you can all get together to compare notes. The Sender can reveal which was the correct picture and you can all see how close you came. If you carry out one test and the Receiver gets the right picture, the chances are 1 in 6 that you were just lucky. But if he gets the right picture twice running, the chances are down to about 3 per cent – and you will have achieved a significant result. The problem is that you can't use the same set of pictures for the second test, because you have all seen them now. So for each test you need to prepare a fresh set of pictures.

How did you get on? If you have been successful you may conclude that telepathy during dreams is possible – as long as you are sure there were no loopholes in your experiment. If you have failed, you may think again about those coincidences between dreams. Next time someone says 'I dreamed the very same thing,' you might just wonder ...

Are All Dreams Merely Figments of the Imagination?

We know that dreams are extraordinary; like Cicero, we should be doubtful about assuming they are therefore paranormal. Look back at the three cases earlier in this chapter.

Mrs Griffith's story is remarkable because her son was so far away, and because she claims she dreamed he was in terrible trouble on the very night that he died. The telephone was not invented until 1875; so she could hardly have had

▶

news any earlier than by letter, which seems to have taken several weeks from West Africa.

The weakness of her story is that it relies entirely on her honesty; there were no witnesses. Had she written down an account of the dream the following morning, and shown that account to someone else, or sent it to be published, then the evidence would have been remarkable. But she might have invented the entire story, long after the event. She might well have elaborated on her experiences of that night – 'remembered them with advantages' as Shakespeare would have said. We have only her word for it that she had a dream at all. She says she told an old servant about it at the time, but we do not know the name of the servant; nor do we have the servant's supporting statement.

Mrs Garrett's story is slightly better supported. She says she wrote down at the time what her daughter said in the dream. Furthermore she sent a telegram to the headmistress; presumably the facts of the case could at the time have been corroborated by the headmistress, and backed up by the telegram itself, and by the subsequent letter from the daughter—although after more than 20 years the evidence may all have disappeared by now.

Even Cicero's dream of the young man is suspect, for he might easily have persuaded himself that the young man he met was the one in his dream. For all we know he may have run into Octavius in a bar the previous night.

The point of keeping your own dream diary and doing controlled experiments is to try to fix the evidence, so that if dream telepathy does work you have a chance of proving it—at least to yourself!

4

Dowsing

Do you believe that people can walk about, finding underground water by holding forked twigs in their hands and watching for the twigs to twitch? Traditionally this is what dowsers or diviners do. The meaning has been extended to include people who find all sorts of things, from oil to gold mines, using an extensive variety of simple equipment.

Many remarkable stories have been told about amazing dowsing successes, but none more remarkable than those of Harry Grattan and Clayton McDowell.

Water for an Army

The years after the end of the Second World War were busy for Colonel Harry Grattan of the British Army's Royal Engineers. He was heavily involved in rebuilding programmes, and the pinnacle of his career came in 1952 when he was given orders to build a huge military base at Rheindalen, near Mönchengladbach in northern Germany. The building was to be paid for with German reparation money, and it had to be completed quickly; within 18 months he had to produce a complete self-contained headquarters for 10,000 soldiers.

He carried off this great challenge with such success that Joint Headquarters Rheindalen was for decades the major NATO defence base in Northern Europe.

One problem Grattan had to solve was the water supply; the base would need three quarters of a million gallons of fresh water every day. To buy this amount would cost at least £20,000 a year. There were three nearby German water-works: at Rheindalen itself, at Uvekoven, and at Waldniel. Each was within about five kilometres of the base, but all three had limited supplies of poor, hard, alkaline water. Furthermore, Grattan was worried that in a time of crisis an enemy might be able to tamper with the supply.

Despite his busy schedule, Grattan decided to tackle this problem himself. He knew that at a hunting lodge in the middle of the site there was a well containing good, soft water. Also, he was confident that he could detect the source of this water by using a dowsing rod. He cut a forked hazel twig in the woods, and went out one Sunday afternoon to walk over the ground.

No sooner had he begun to walk than he felt a strong downward pull; he was sure there was water underground. He felt the pull over most of the centre of the site. There was no surface water; so the rod suggested a water-bearing 'sandwich' beneath the surface. He decided that if this supply was to be of any real use he would have to find out how far it stretched. The camp covered many acres of land; so he took to his horse and found to his delight that dowsing seemed to be equally effective from the saddle.

Every evening he rode out into the Hardt Forest, ranging far and wide across the country, and carefully logged his results. He found the pull of 'his' water extended almost to all three German waterworks, but astonishingly each of them seemed to be supplied by a separate source, for there was a 'dead' area with no water between the 'sandwich' he had found and each of theirs. He found that the surface feature of the Schwalm Stream had no effect on his water 'sandwich', which must therefore be quite deep.

Eventually, after some arm-twisting, he persuaded his bosses to let him drill test bore-holes, and found, in a gravel layer between 73 and 96 feet below the surface, copious amounts of pure, soft, acid water – much better than anything the German waterworks could offer.

The water that Col Harry Grattan found by dowsing from his horse has supplied an army of 10,000 soldiers for more than 40 years.

Clayton McDowell

West Salem, Illinois, is a small town in the Midwest of the United States, about 300 miles south of Chicago. The endless flat fields are full of soya beans and corn – and some of them also boast the 'nodding donkeys' or pump jacks that bring oil to the surface.

This is not rich oil country, however. The wells will never rival those in the giant oil fields of Texas and Oklahoma, although if one person finds and drills several successful wells, he or she can make a good deal of money.

Clayton McDowell lives with his wife Marge on Route 1, just outside town. There are 'his and hers' Cadillacs parked in front, and 170 trotting horses in what they call the backyard. At a recent sale one of the horses fetched $30,000; Clayton and Marge are doing OK.

Ask him where it all comes from, and Clayton produces his nylon dowsing rods – slippery and strong, Y-shaped, with a translucent cylinder of golden crystals at the business end.

He has three rods: one for salt water, one for gas, and one for oil. The oil rod has brought his greatest triumphs. In one year he drilled 33 wells, and found oil in 30 of them. The best was on the grounds of Edwards County Senior High School. Principal Bob Wallace said that money had been very tight, and they had had difficulty getting enough books and equipment for the students, but with an income of $500 a day from the well that Clayton drilled right next to the base-ball diamond, the school's prospects were looking good. 'It was like a gift from God,' said Wallace.

Clayton used to dowse on foot, but like Harry Grattan he found this rather hard work over a large area. Besides, as a young man Clayton lost a leg after being shot in a bar-room fight. Dowsing one day in winter, when the mud was thick as chocolate pie, he almost lost his wooden leg in the mud. Now he takes it easier, and dowses from his Cadillac.

When he feels the urge he turns the Caddy into a field and drives across country. Marge takes the wheel and he gets out the dowsing rod. Bumping slowly over the fields they go, until suddenly the end of the rod seems to dip inexo-rably down, a faint twinkle comes into Clayton's eye, and he knows just where he wants to drill his next well.

Marge is both amused and bemused. She can't dowse: 'The rods won't work for me,' she says. But according to Clayton, only one thing can pull the golden crystals down like that – good clean oil.

Theories of How Dowsing Might Work

Some dowsers search for water, oil, buried treasure, or miner-als; others seek out lost pets, or good investments on the stock exchange. Some work with bent coat-hangers or welding rods; others prefer the pendulum (see Chapter 5) or a piece of bone. These varying methods may work in different ways, but any broad theory of dowsing should be able to explain what makes a forked twig apparently twitch over underground water.

Imagine a dowser walking through a field. Suddenly her hazel rod twitches and dances in her hands. She stops, and marks the spot. Later an underground stream is found beneath the turf.

How could the rod have twitched? There was no visible connection – no piece of string from the underground stream to the rod; no pipe bringing pressure up to pull the rod down.

What about a direct but invisible connection? Pieces of untreated wood tend to bend or 'warp' if they are left outside in the damp. A dramatic example of this is the cathedral spire at Chesterfield, which was built from unweathered oak timbers, and is now twisted like a corkscrew. This warping force can be strong, but it acts extremely slowly; it usually takes at least several hours, and often several weeks. By contrast the dowsing reaction is fast; the twig twitches and jumps – it often shows a large movement in less than a second. This can hardly be the same process in action.

To bring about such a dramatic movement there appears to be some action at a distance – a phenomenon that works through space.

Action at a Distance

There are two well-known phenomena that cause force to be exerted at a distance – gravity and magnetism. The force of gravity pulls things towards the centre of the Earth, and extends from there not merely to the surface, where it gives us weight, and as high as the mountaintops (for snow falls on them) but right across the universe; gravity holds galaxies together. But there is no reason to suppose that the force of gravity is altered by the presence or absence of water underground, and no one has succeeded in measuring any such effect. Furthermore, if the dowsing reaction were due to gravity, then dowsers would find the densest materials most easily – and lead is not high on their list of claimed successes.

What about magnetism? Could that be the answer? Many people think so. Certainly most metals cause disturbances in the local magnetic field, which can be detected by scientific instruments or by a compass. You can try this out for yourself. Take a simple compass – the kind with a needle that points north – and move it close to a pair of scissors or a spoon, or any other chunk of metal. Then try moving it over some non-metallic objects. You can easily find out which metals and other substances are magnetic and which are not.

Distorting the Earth's Magnetic Field

The Earth itself behaves like a giant magnet and all over the surface we can detect the magnetic field – not very strong, but enough to make a compass needle point towards the north pole. Lumps of metal bend and distort this magnetic field, just like a nearly-finished dam distorts the flow of a stream. The water is funnelled through the gap at great speed, just as the magnetic field is funnelled through the metal.

Because lumps of metal disturb the Earth's magnetic field, they are often detectable by means of a compass – or a metal detector. Perhaps that is the basis of the dowsing reaction too.

There are two substantial problems. First, water is not magnetic. The most sensitive scientific instruments can scarcely detect the difference between ground with water underneath and ground without. How can a dowsing rod be better?

Second, the hazel twig is not magnetic either, and apparently cannot respond even to the strongest magnetic field. So how can it detect a change in field too weak for the most sensitive instruments?

Animal Magnetism?

Perhaps the answer lies in the fact that some *people* are sensitive to magnetic fields. This is not well understood, but some people think it provides a clue.

Homing pigeons can be released hundreds of miles from their homes, and still find their way back within hours. Close to home they probably recognize landmarks, but from far afield they somehow have to decide which way to fly. One theory is that they set a course by the sun, knowing from an internal clock what time of day it is, and therefore being able to work out roughly whether to fly with the sun on their right or their left. Another theory is that they can detect the polarization of the sunlight.

Other people suggest that pigeons are sensitive to magnetic fields and can therefore calculate which way to fly in roughly the same way that we would use a compass.

People also have a significant skill in orientation. Experiments have been done in which groups of people have been blindfolded and then driven many miles in a bus, around a twisting route. Then they are all invited to get off the bus, in a place they don't know, and point towards their home. They turn out to be remarkably good at choosing the right direction; so perhaps people too are sensitive to magnetic fields.

But even if the dowsers are sensitive to magnetic fields, this still doesn't provide an explanation for dowsing. Unless the objects they are searching for cause changes in the magnetic field this is not going to help them. Perhaps we need to look in a completely different direction.

Dowsing Rods Are Amplifiers

Dowsing equipment comes in many shapes and sizes, but it all has one thing in common. Every dowsing rod is an unstable mechanical amplifier.

A pencil balanced on its end on the table is an unstable mechanical amplifier; the slightest jog will make it fall over. Thus a tiny movement of the table is amplified to become a big movement of the pencil. This is how dowsing rods work. The traditional forked twig is held in tension with the thumbs pressing outwards, so that a slight movement or twitch makes the forked end jump upwards or downwards. Try making it move with your fingers and you will find that only the slightest tremor is enough to make the rod jump. The same goes for L-rods made from coat-hangers.

Now we may have the beginning of an explanation. Dowsing rods amplify very slight signals – but where does the signal come from? There are just two main possibilities. Either there is truly something magical about dowsing and the signal is some kind of mysterious energy as yet unknown to science – or it is something perfectly normal. Perhaps the dowser already knows, subconsciously, where the water (or gold or oil) is. Then the dowsing rods could amplify that subconscious knowledge (or psychic awareness) and make it visible. The dowser need not be aware that she already knows the answer. So as far as she is concerned the twig moves all by itself.

But where does the subconscious knowledge come from?

The Lie of the Land

The young John D. Rockefeller is said to have stood in the wide open spaces of the United States in the 1860s and listened to the haunting sounds of the railroad. As each train thundered across the prairie, the engine note would change once in a while, as the gradient of the track varied. After much practice, Rockefeller was able to use these changes in pitch to predict where oil would be found beneath the surface, and he made millions of dollars as a result.

Many seekers of water have become highly skilled in spotting small changes in vegetation in places where water is to be found. Sometimes the ground may be swampy.

Sometimes the clues may be much less obvious; there may be a change in the colour of the grass, or merely a different type of moss or lichen growing on the rocks. Or the pattern of rocks and soil may change. Often such experience is hard to describe in words, and the water diviner will say he can 'smell' where to dig a well. Perhaps sometimes he can.

Suppose he carries a forked twig, and unconsciously noticing the change in grass colour causes his thumbs to twitch, and the rod dips down. They dig and find water. Who can tell whether the rod dipped because of a change in the magnetic field, or because the dowser subconsciously knew because of the grass that there was likely to be water under that spot?

There are many things we learn, through our lives, and yet cannot put into words. We meet people whom we instinctively dislike, and we have good or bad feelings about places we visit. These 'intuitions' may well be valid, at least some of the time. Somehow our brains have put together all of our experience and got a general impression of what sort of people are trustworthy or generous, what sorts of places are dangerous or safe. We cannot consciously say 'people with slightly smaller eyes, closer together, are meaner than people with big noses and sticking-out ears', but there may be some judgment like this underlying what we have learned.

Some people have powerful intuitions and can annoy the rest of us by being so often right – but probably they do it by this long accumulation of learning. It may be just the same with the lie of the land. A good dowser may not be able consciously to say what he knows. It takes the dowsing rods to amplify that buried knowledge.

We now have three possible theories to explain dowsing. One – there is some mysterious force on the rods; two – your mind makes deductions from information you already have in your subconscious; and three – your mind picks up hidden information by some psychic process. How can you find out which is right? If you want to find out for yourself, the first step is to learn how to dowse.

How to Dowse

Anybody can learn to dowse. You need only two things – a little equipment and a lot of practice.

You can buy dowsing rods in specialist occult shops, but it is better to make your own – not only because it costs less but because you can fiddle about until you have something that feels just right for you.

Cutting a Forked Twig

The traditional implement for dowsing is a hazel twig, and there is a lot of superstition about how, when, and where it has to be cut.

I was once instructed to go walking in the fields until I found a tree that felt just right, then to walk around it slowly, seven times, 'widdershins' – that is, anti-clockwise – all the time thinking about the use to which I was going to put the twigs. Only then was I to take out my knife and cut a Y-shaped twig of just the right thickness.

But this is nothing to the complicated procedure some have advised. An eighteenth-century *grimoire,* or magical text, commands the wouldbe magician to cut his hazel wand with one blow of a consecrated dagger at the moment of sunrise, saying, 'I pluck thee in the name of Eloim, Muthraton, Adonay and Semiphoras, that by their power thou mayest possess the virtues of the rod of Moses, for the discovery of all that I desire to know.'

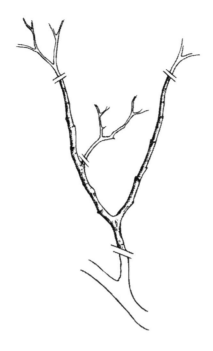

Figure 4.1: A good dowsing twig should have equal branches, about 30 cm (1 ft) long. The branch below the fork should be slightly thinner than the width of your little finger (about 1 cm or ½ an inch).

You may think this is a load of rubbish – surely it cannot matter what words you say – nor whether it is exactly sunrise or not! But to think this is to forget the powers of our own minds. Perhaps going through a long and precise ritual puts you into the right frame of mind for dowsing. The words themselves might not matter. You could mutter 'In the name of Persil, Omo, Bold, and Safeway's own brand' if you were convinced it would help. But this is just speculation; don't take my word for it. If you want to find out whether it really does matter, you need to do some experiments. And the first thing is to learn how to dowse.

Fortunately most modern dowsers do not use complicated rituals. You may cut your twig without further ceremony.

Hazel is traditional, and it has just about the right springiness. We have also made useful twigs from hawthorn, ash, and a bush in the garden that we can't identify. Look for a twig that divides into two roughly equal branches and is a bit thinner than your little finger (1 cm/ ½ in or less). Take a sharp knife or (easier) secateurs and find a place where it divides into two roughly equal branches. Cut it as shown in Figure 4.2. If you have found a thick hazel bush or hedge you may like to cut two or three to try out. Do try to find forks with equally thick branches, for holding the twig is more difficult when one side is bendier than the other.

Figure 4.2: When cutting your dowsing twig, look for a fork with branches of equal thickness, and don't worry about side-shoots – you can trim them off.

Holding a Forked Twig

The main task is to learn to grasp the twig correctly. Place your hands close together in front of you, palms up and thumbs outwards. Rest the branches of your twig across your fingers. Bend your fingers up to hold them, then press the ends gently away from you with your thumbs. If you have cut a good springy twig you will feel the pressure. Now you simply have to keep the point of the Y facing forwards while you hold the branches firmly.

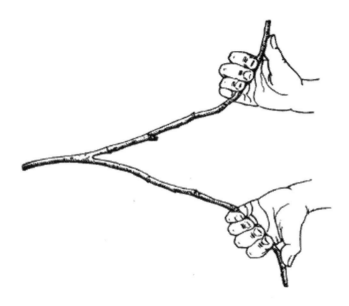

Figure 4.3: Hold the dowsing twig horizontally with your palms up, pushing the ends out with your thumbs, and pulling the fork back towards you with your fingers.

Holding the twig like this, walk about the house, or preferably in the garden, a park, or over fields – or even in the street if you don't mind being stared at. You will soon find that your Y-shaped twig does not keep steady all the time. Sometimes it will suddenly jump, dipping down or flicking up towards you. This is what you are looking for – the 'dowsing reaction'. Practise using your twig until you are used to its sudden jumps and tugs. Notice when and where it happens and try to get a feel for how it behaves.

Figure 4.4: (a) Walk with your twig at about waist height, forearms horizontal; (b) When you get a dowsing reaction, the twig will twist sharply upwards or downwards.

Metal Rods

Many modern dowsers prefer to use simple L-shaped angle rods. You can buy these, but again it is simple and cheap to make your own. Some people insist that they must be made from copper – if you like you can buy thin copper rods for the purpose, or try to borrow some copper welding rods from a welder. However, the humble wire coat-hanger makes a per-fectly good pair of angle rods.

Using a pair of pliers, cut off the hook and twizzled part of the wire. Straighten out the rest as well as you can, and cut two equal rods about 40 cm/16 in long (anything from 30–50 cm/12–20 in will do). Bend down the end of each one at right angles to make a short arm of about 10 cm (4 in). Your rods are ready.

This method uses only one hanger, but you have to straighten out four bends. If you have two spare hangers it is easier to make one rod from each of them.

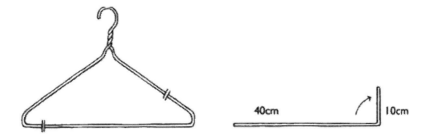

Figure 4.5: Use pliers to cut a simple L-rod from a wire coat-hanger. Alternatively, you can make two L-rods from one hanger by cutting just below the twist and in the middle of the straight section – but then you have to straighten out four bends.

To use the L-rods hold them by the shorter segment – like pistols – and practise walking around with both the long ends pointing forwards. You will find that as you walk about the ends will tend suddenly to move wide apart, or come together and cross over. With metal rods, this swinging wide or crossing over is the desired 'dowsing reaction'. Once again walk around until you feel comfortable with your reacting rods.

Some dowsers say they get better results by dropping the short arms into the plastic cases of old ballpoint pens. This is supposed to make the friction more uniform than it is if you hold them in your hands. We do not find these plastic hold-ers particularly helpful, but they may work for you.

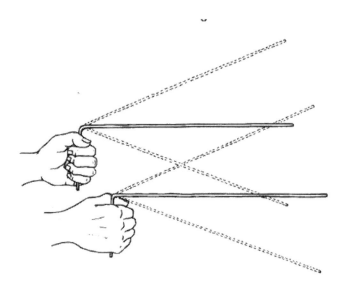

Figure 4.6: Hold the L-rods like a pair of pistols in front of you, hands close together at waist height. In a dowsing reaction they will swing suddenly inwards or outwards.

Trying Out your Equipment

When you have made your forked twig or metal rods, and learned how to walk with them, try a simple test. Run some water in a washing-up bowl, in a bucket, in the kitchen sink or in a bath. Or go out and try over a pond or stream. Holding out your twig or rods, walk forward until your hands are over the water. Do you get a dowsing reaction? If so, you are ready for some experiments.

Perhaps you have found that the twigs seem to 'work' for you. They twist and turn in your hands, jump at significant places, and do so without your making any effort. But does this really mean that you can find things with them? It is time to test your new-found powers and find out whether they come from the twigs or from your own mind, and whether by psychic powers or not.

A Simple Dowsing Test

A simple test is to get a friend to hide a coin under the carpet and see whether you can find it just by walking to and fro with your twig or rods. Naturally you should go out of the room while the coin is being hidden.

This kind of test is fun – and good practice for you – but it won't really establish whether or not dowsing is really a mysterious power. You can probably think of reasons why this is not a good enough test. For example, you could have heard your friend walking about while she hid the coin or, if she was in the room with you while you were dowsing, she might have given you some subtle clue as to where it was. You might think of other reasons why this is not foolproof. To investigate dowsing properly we need a better test.

Figure 4.7: Some experts say the friction and the results are more consistent if you support the rods in the plastic cases of old ballpoint pens.

Scientific Dowsing Test

Here is one that you can easily carry out at home, in the house or – better still – in the garden. The aim of this experiment is to find out whether dowsing works all the time, or only when you already know the answer. To do this you need to compare an 'open test', in which you know the answer, with a 'closed test' in which you do not. Can you succeed in them both?

What You Need

- 6 similar containers for water (if they are identical so much the better). Buckets are ideal, but you may not have six buckets! Try large plastic flower pots, with a plastic bag full of water in one of them; or use saucepans or yogurt pots. Write numbers on them, or place numbered pieces of paper underneath them.
- 6 lids to cover them with. They must cover the containers completely so that you cannot possibly see inside. Try plates, or saucepan lids.
- A die.
- Two friends to be Experimenter and Assistant. Decide in advance who is to do which job.
- Score Sheets. Make your own, or copy the one given below.
- You (the Dowser) and your twigs or rods.

Procedure 1 : The Open Test

Ask your Assistant to line up the buckets and fill just one with water. Leaving the lids off, walk along the line holding your hands over each one in turn, while your Assistant marks down whether the twigs respond or not. You will have to decide between you what counts as a 'response'.

Mark the results on the Score Sheet for 'open test'.

Do the twigs respond? If they jump at every bucket, even the empty ones, then you may need more practice – or you may not be cut out to be a dowser. But if they respond only to the one with water in and not to the others, then you can carry on. You now know that the twigs respond to water, but you do not know whether this is because you can see the water. The next test will establish this.

Dowsing Scoresheet

Mark dowser's choice 0, and the correct answer √

Open test

Container

	1	2	3	4	5	6
Trial 1						
2						
3						
4						
5						

Total Correct_____

Closed test

Container

	1	2	3	4	5	6
Trial 1						
2						
3						
4						
5						

Total Correct_____

Procedure 2: The Closed Test

The *Experimenter's* job is to choose which container will contain water in each trial, and then set it up secretly. Prepare for five trials. Use a die to decide which bucket to fill on each trial. This is important, because if you pick the buckets yourself the Dowser might easily guess your choices.

Find a quiet place well away from the Dowser and the Assistant and throw the die five times. Write down the numbers you get; for example, 1, 4, 4, 4, 3. These will be the numbers of the buckets that will have later in each trial. Keep this list secret until the experiment is done.

Now fill the bucket indicated for trial 1. Put on all the lids. Check that no water has spilled, or can be seen, and that there is no way your Dowser will be able to see which contains water.

Tell the Assistant you are ready. You must now go away, because you are the only person who knows which bucket contains water, and you might give the game away!

The *Assistant's* job is to ask the Dowser to walk along the row, watch the reactions of the twigs, and get the Dowser to decide which bucket contains the water. If the twigs or rods do not respond at all, keep trying. If they respond to more than one bucket keep on going until you can decide which gets the strongest reaction.

Mark the answer down on the Score Sheet for 'closed test' *(see page 83). You must write down the result of every trial. Do not leave some out because they don't work well. After you have written down the choice,* you may both look in the bucket to see whether the choice was right.

You and the Dowser now go out of sight and hearing while the Experimenter prepares for the next trial.

Carry out four more trials in the same way.

You must ensure that the Experimenter, who knows which bucket has water in, is not around when you perform the test. It is easy to give away clues when you don't mean to.

When you have finished all five trials, you can all get together. Compare the list of which buckets had water in with the Dowser's answers.

How many were right?

How many would you expect to be right by chance?

The Results

With six buckets you have a 1-in-6 chance of being right each time; so you are likely to get one right roughly every six times you try. So it is quite likely that you will get at least one right in five trials. The results become interesting only when you get most of them right.

To help you work out how significant your findings are, below there is a simple table of probabilities. Look up how many trials you did and how many you got right. The table will tell you the odds against getting that many just by chance. You may get more extreme odds if you do more trials, but make sure you *keep the results for every single trial.* It is no good throwing away the results for the ones that don't succeed.

DOWSING – the percentage chance of getting it right

Number of trials	→		1	2	3	4	5
Number correct	0		83	69	58	48	40
	1		17	28	35	39	40
	2			3	7	12	16
	3				0.5	1.5	3
	4					0.1	0.3
	5						0.01

To get a result that professional researchers would call 'significant', you need to get a score that proves you had a less than 5 per cent chance that you were just lucky.

Conclusion

How did you do? Did you do as well with the lids on as with them off? If so, you are really demonstrating some strange powers.

Did you succeed with the lids off but not with them on? If so, there is a strong possibility that your dowsing power comes not from a direct connection between the twigs and the water, but from your own mind.

What do you think? Have your experiments helped you understand dowsing?

Problems with the Experiment

You may have thought up some of the problems yourself. If there were any way you could have detected which bucket contained the water your results would not be valid. Did you kick or touch any of the buckets as you went past? Were there drops of water lying about? Could the Experimenter have given you any clues?

If you think this experiment is not good enough you might think up better ones of your own.

Further Experiments

Do your twigs respond to jewellery? Money? Crystals? If so, you can do the experiment in the same way. Using a set of identical small containers – yogurt pots with lids, for example – you could dowse for money by placing a coin in one of the containers.

Once again, try the test when you can see inside the containers, and then again when you cannot. What do you think of your powers now? Could you get rich finding money this way? Could you do better than a metal detector on the beach or in a park?

Some dowsers claim to be able to be able to detect electricity. Their twigs respond when they walk over wires or cables that are 'live', but not otherwise.

You might now be able to devise a test for this claim too. Do your twigs respond only when there is electricity flowing in your test wire? You will have to ensure that there is no obvious way of you knowing whether the wire is 'live' or not.

Using ideas from the first experiment you may be able to devise a clever one of your own.

In the end what do you conclude? Does dowsing work directly on the rods, or through the diviner's mind? And if you agree with our conclusion that it is all in the mind, can *you* devise experiments to show whether the mind is acting on information already stored subconsciously, or by some direct psychic connection with the target?

Is It All True?

There is undoubtedly a dowsing reaction, but does it come from the twigs, the fingers, or the brain? That question is hard to untangle. Dowsing practitioners are convinced they have a gift, and point to hundreds of dowsing successes, but rarely mention their failures.

In 1970, the Military Engineering Experimental Establishment (MEXE) set up one of the most elaborate and well-organized dowsing trials of all time. They commandeered 400 acres of heathland, and set to work.

First they tried map-dowsing. They buried 20 mines, and then invited a small group of dowsers to find them, using a map of the area. The dowsers were less accurate than a second group of volunteers who merely guessed where the mines were buried.

Then the experimenters bulldozed flat a section of heath, and dug 400 holes in a grid, 20 feet apart. In the holes, according to a preplanned pattern, one group of soldiers buried 160 mines, another buried chunks of concrete, a third chunks of wood, and a fourth just plain earth. Some of the mines were metallic, others plastic. No one person knew

▶

---

where everything was located; the master plan was kept locked in a safe.

They asked for more dowsers, and 22 turned up on the day to try their skill. They used metal rods, wooden rods, nylon rods, and a pendulum. All day they toiled to and fro across the bulldozed heath, searching for the mines.

Alas they did no better than chance. One dowser missed 142 of the 160 mines. Another found 147 of them – but then he also found 'mines' in 185 other squares.

Because all 400 holes had been dug, and then refilled, and the ground had been bulldozed, the dowsers in this MEXE trial were deprived of all the clues that might normally have been available – and they failed to find the mines. This may not prove (or disprove) anything, but it does suggest that the skill of dowsing starts mainly in the mind of the diviner.

5

The Pendulum

When we visited the annual convention of the American Society of Dowsers (ASD) in Danville, Vermont, there were pendulums everywhere. They were being used by old men, middle-aged women and young children, and most of the users were convinced that their pendulums somehow tuned them in to the universe.

When I went down to breakfast I found an elderly woman swinging a pendulum over her breakfast muffins. When I asked why, she said that the pendulum told her whether they were good to eat, wholesome and digestible.

When I went to the grocery store, I found the ASD's secretary working with her pendulum over the fruit and vegetables. She explained that she found it much more effective than a thumb in picking out those that were ripe and unbruised. I like to *feel* melons and avocados, to find ones that are just beginning to soften. I like to look for bruises on the apples and make sure the tomatoes are not overripe. Apparently the pendulum is more sensitive than my fingers and my eyes.

The most remarkable story we heard in Danville was from Rose Marie and George Chelekis, a young couple who had laid flooring down in their loft. The area was quite big, and they had worked hard for many hours to nail the boards down on to the rafters. When they had finished they relaxed downstairs, and George went to make a phone call – only to find that the phone was out of action.

He knew at once what the problem was. The phone lines lay in the roof space; he must have driven a nail through the wire and caused a short circuit. The difficulty now was that they had put about 2,000 nails into the boards; which one went through the phone wire?

Up he went to dowse the loft space. He divided it up into about 10 areas and in each one he asked the question 'Is the short in this area?' This gave him one area to work in. Then Rose Marie took over and, using her pendulum, eliminated all but one section of board, and within five minutes was down to a single nail.

She pulled out the nail – and the phone worked perfectly.

An Instrument of Many Uses

Some people claim they can find distant objects – buried treasure, minerals or oil – by using a pendulum and a map. They will spread the map out on a table, swing the pendulum over it, and then ask for whatever it is they want to find.

Other people use pendulums to help them take decisions. 'Should I go to the party tonight?' or 'What is the best place to go shopping?' I have even heard assertions that the pendulum is the only effective way to choose between two possible lovers. Ask the pendulum and let it take the decision. After all, if it really is tuned in to the Universe, it may be better informed than you are.

Pendulums have been used to diagnose illness, to prescribe medicine, by American marines to search for hidden Vietcong guerrilla fighters and by the German High Command to scour the oceans for British and American warships.

One of the most spectacular successes of all time was achieved during the Second World War by oil wild-catter Ace Gutowski and farmer J. W. Young. Their pendulum was a bottle covered in goatskin, filled with a mysterious secret fluid and hanging from a watch chain. They called it a 'doodlebug'.

When Ace followed the pendulum's lead and drilled in West Edmond – dull, flat country just a few miles northwest of Oklahoma City – he discovered what turned out to be the largest oil-field of all time, in what had been thought an unpromising geological area. There was a serious oil shortage in 1944, and his find was of major importance to the United States' war effort. The press headlines were spectacular:

GUTOWSKI FINDS OCEAN OF CRUDE!

The Origins of Pendulum Power

People have probably been using pendulums ever since they had enough time to sit and think, and fix long hairs to pebbles – but there may be some truth in the theory that the spiritual use of pendulums follows the nineteenth-century magical practice known as 'the ring and the disc'.

A magician would suspend a gold ring on a silk thread over a parchment disc, on which would be inscribed the words

YES and NO

Then he would invoke the power of the spirit and ask questions about the future, about what sort of sacrifice was needed, or about whether or not the accused was guilty. By the swing of the ring over the disc, the answer would be revealed.

Would you like your guilt or innocence to be established this way? Is it fair to punish someone or let them off according to the swing of the pendulum? The fact is people have often used such devices in the absence of anything better. But does the pendulum work at all?

The first step in finding out is to learn to use the pendulum yourself.

Making your Own Pendulum

You need only a piece of string and a small weight to act as the 'bob'.

The materials you use are probably not important, but if you can make a pleasing pendulum you will enjoy working with it.

In our experience the thinner the string the better, and also the more slippery the better. So the worst to use would be thick stiff rope. The best would be strong black cotton, silk thread, or finely braided nylon string. But you may prefer the warm textured feel of a piece of knitting wool. The choice is up to you. Try several types of string and see which you prefer. You will need a total length between 30 and 45 cm (12 and 18 in). When you hold your pendulum the bob should be between 10 and 30 cm (4 and 12 in) below your hand.

The bob should be dense – a piece of polished wood, a pebble, a crystal, a piece of glass or metal, or perhaps a gold ring. Some pendulum experts like to use a ring with sentimental value – granny's wedding ring, for example. A pendant, perhaps one earring, can be simple and effective. Whatever you use, the mass should be about 10–20 grams (½ oz), and ideally the bob should have a pointer at the bottom so that you can see exactly what it is pointing at – on a map, for example.

Some experts say that beginners should start with a heavier bob – perhaps 60–100 g (2–3 oz), and perhaps a slightly longer string. More massive bobs are less likely to be influenced by stray draughts, which can be important if you plan to use your pendulum out of doors.

For the simplest bob of all, just to try out the technique, you could use a lump of plasticine squeezed over the end of the string, and shaped to a point underneath.

At the top of the string it is convenient to tie a loop big enough to slip two fingers into. This makes the pendulum simple to hold and use. There can be more of a problem fixing the string to the bob. Using an old ring is an easy solution, since you can simply tie the string to the ring. If you are a knot enthusiast, try an anchor bend for this, or a bowline. Otherwise, use any knot you know how to tie.

If you are using a crystal or a pebble, try first a lump of Bluetack and see whether this is strong enough to hold the weight of the bob. Try the pendulum out over a cushion or other soft surface, so the bob won't get damaged if it falls. Provided you are happy with this combination of string and bob, you can either tie the string into a cradle or sling for the bob, or fasten the string directly to the bob with a dab of glue.

Figure 5.1: A ring makes a good pendulum bob. You can easily tie a piece of thread or string round it.

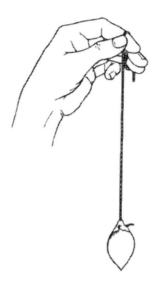

Figure 5.2: You can try out your pendulum first with a piece of Bluetack.

A more elegant solution is to glue to the bob a small circle of wire, to which you can tie your string later. One advantage is that you should be able to get the bob pointing downwards – by gluing the wire ring at the top.

Trying Out your Pendulum

Now you have your pendulum, you can try it out. Put the loop over your second or third finger, or both, and hold the string below the loop between thumb and forefinger. Let the bob hang. At first it will probably spin as the string untwists. This will sort itself out after 30 seconds or so; for this process you can hang it from a hook or doorhandle if you wish.

Then hold the pendulum out at arm's length, and try to keep your hand completely steady. Concentrate on your hand, and on keeping your fingers motionless.

Within a few seconds the bob will probably begin to move. First it may sway irregularly from side to side. The swaying may become more regular. Then it may turn into a circular movement – the bob may begin to swing in circles, either clockwise or anti-clockwise. You are beginning to get in tune with your pendulum.

If you don't find the pendulum moving easily, it may be that you are trying too hard. One of the legendary gurus of the pendulum, the Swiss Abbé Mermet who during the 1920s and 1930s allegedly had the skill with a pendulum to find not merely water but also gold and missing children, advised the novice 'Don't try to *will* your pendulum to move, just imagine it moving.'

First Steps

Once your pendulum is moving, your first task is to learn what the various movements mean. The simplest is just a straight swing to and fro, in a straight line towards you and away from you. Can you persuade your pendulum to do this?

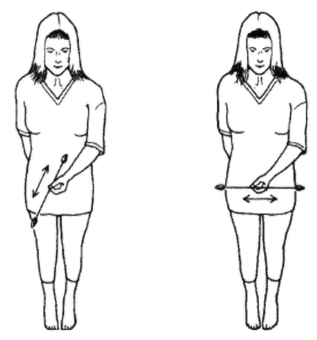

Figure 5.3: The pendulum swinging (a) to and fro in the 'neutral' position and (b) left and right to indicate a response.

Some people just think, *'Forwards, backwards, forwards, backwards'* to themselves, to encourage the pendulum to move in this way. Some focus on the bob, and try to influence it by direct mind-power. Others speak to it aloud, and command it to move in this line. If you feel silly speaking aloud, do it under your breath.

This may take some practice, but within half an hour you should find the pendulum will swing most of the time in that one line, to and fro.

Many experts regard this as the natural 'zero position' of the pendulum. Getting the bob to stay still is tricky, and they prefer to start all their work from this neutral to-and-fro swing.

Once you have mastered the to-and-fro swing, encourage the bob to move in a straight line from left to right and back again.

Again, with practice you should be able to make it go from to-and-fro to left-and-right, and then back to to-and-fro. Keep your hand as still as you can and focus on the movement of the bob. If you run into difficulties, remember Abbé Mermet's advice.

When you are confident about both the to-and-fro and left-and-right movements of the pendulum, you are ready to move on to circles. Focus on your bob and get it to move, first in a clockwise circle and then in an anti-clockwise circle.

Spend at least a day or two practising all these four movements. When you can produce any one of them at will, you are ready to put your pendulum to use.

Yes and No

The simplest way, and perhaps the most popular among pendulum experts is to 'train' your pendulum to indicate 'Yes' and 'No'.

You may choose how to do this, but a simple system is to decide that a clockwise circle means 'Yes' and an anti-clockwise circle means 'No'.

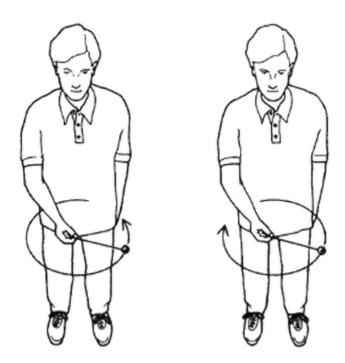

Figure 5.4: Ask your pendulum a question. (a) Clockwise means 'Yes'. (b) Anti-clockwise means 'No'.

You must decide whether this is right for you. Once you have decided, you must train your pendulum. Say 'Clockwise means Yes' over and over again, while willing your pendulum to move clockwise. When you have this working, will it to move anti-clockwise, saying 'Anti-clockwise means No' over and over.

Then test it by starting at a neutral position – perhaps the to-and-fro swing – and then saying 'Yes! – Show me Yes.' The pendulum should then move clockwise.

Once you and your pendulum are 'trained', you can begin to ask it questions:

Should I eat this muffin for breakfast?

Should I buy this melon?

Should I have one spoonful of sugar in my tea?

You must keep the questions simple, and make sure they can be answered with a Yes or No. If you ask 'What is the weather going to be like tomorrow?' you won't get anywhere! As long as you keep the questions simple, you can now ask your pendulum anything.

Note: Some people prefer to think of clockwise as meaning TRUE and anti-clockwise meaning FALSE. This is much the same as Yes and No; use TRUE and FALSE if you are happy with these words. But then to consult your pendulum you must make statements such as 'I am doing the right thing to eat this muffin for breakfast' or 'I should buy this melon'–in each case expecting the answer TRUE or FALSE.

How Could Pendulums Work?

Some books claim that pendulums are in tune with the natural forces of the Universe, which sounds powerful but does not explain how they work, nor how they can answer questions.

One text claims that in the hands of a trained operator 'the pendulum reads exact energy patterns, which in the final analysis, is the only truth we know.' I find this hard to understand. I don't know what an 'exact energy pattern' is, and it certainly isn't the only truth I know. Nor is there any suggestion of how the pendulum can read these energy patterns. This is quite unlike, say, a thermometer or a light meter; I do understand how those instruments use the energy of heat or light to produce a reading.

Some practitioners have called their art 'radiesthesia', which suggests that the pendulum is controlled by some sort of radiation. The idea is that all objects give off radiation – and if the pendulum, or the human body holding it, can tune in to this radiation – like a TV set tunes in to various channels – then the radiesthetist can pick up whatever he or she is looking for. There are several problems with this theory, however.

One problem is that the main radiation emitted by most things is heat; the amount depends on their temperature. So all melons on the same supermarket shelf will emit the same heat radiation, because they are all at the same temperature. The ripe ones will be indistinguishable from the others.

Melons and most other objects also reflect light rays, and the variations in these produce the colour of the object. But our eyes are good at detecting colour; so if we wanted to choose melons by colour – which is probably a good way to do it – then our eyes will be more effective than pendulums.

Another difficulty is that pendulums are supposed to help with abstract problems, such as diagnosis of disease. How can a disease emit radiation? Someone with a high temperature will certainly emit more heat, but you would be better off using a thermometer to measure his or her temperature.

Even harder to understand is the idea of map dowsing. How could the various squares on a map give off different kinds of radiation?

We would like to find scientific reasons to explain the pendulum's curious behaviour – and it is certainly curious.

What Makes the Pendulum Swing?

Try hanging your pendulum from a fixed object – a hook, a peg, a doorhandle or the back of a chair. Leave it for a minute or so to stop spinning, steady it with your finger, and then leave it for another minute.

Now, without touching it or whatever it is tied to, try to influence it to swing in the basic to-and-fro line. Try any of the other simple motions. Can you make it move?

We have tried this experiment several times, and we have been unable to make it swing. It simply hangs there, leaden, unresponsive, stationary.

1. *Observation 1:* The pendulum swings when held by finger and thumb.
2. *Observation 2:* The pendulum does not swing when hung on a peg, hook or doorhandle.
3. *Conclusion:* There is something special about the finger and thumb.

Experiments have shown that even the calmest of us cannot keep our hands completely still. Try it yourself. Hold out your hands at arm's length – your fingers will always be moving. If you think you are doing well, try holding a pencil horizontal in each hand, points towards one another. Now just touch the points together, and hold them there. The pencils seem to have a life of their own; holding the points so that they just touch is extremely difficult.

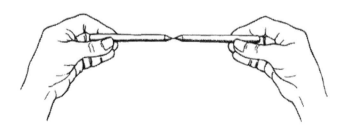

Figure 5.5: Can you do this? Hold two pencils at arm's length, keeping the tips just touching.

The muscles that move your arms, wrists and fingers are controlled by hundreds of nerves, and the precise way the nerves fire is controlled by special centres in the brain. To move your finger an inch sideways the brain sends off a whole battery of nerve signals to make the muscles move. It then gets messages back from the muscles to tell it how much they've moved. If you are also *looking* at your finger, the brain gets signals from the eyes to tell it where the finger is. This is much more accurate and explains why it helps to look whenever you want to make a skilled movement.

Holding your hand out at arm's length needs hundreds of instructions to separate muscles, which are working against one another, some trying to lift your hand up, some trying to lower it. Every time the hand drifts away from the desired position, the nerves fire to try to get it back again.

Riding a bicycle is easier when you are moving. You certainly can't sit upright on a stationary bike. You just fall off. But when the bike is moving along you can easily compensate for a slight tilt one way by leaning or moving the handlebars that way and correcting for the tilt. Once you have learned to ride a bike you never forget – and you do all the correcting automatically. You don't have to think, 'Help, I'm leaning to the left; I need to make a quick corrective movement.' Your nerves and muscles do it without your conscious control.

Even standing upright is like this. You don't stand perfectly still but sway slightly in every direction. As you move, the nerves fire and order the muscles to put you upright again. This way, with constant very slight movements, you end up more or less still.

These slight movements are what makes the pencil points hard to hold together, and also what makes the pendulum move when you hold it. The pendulum swings not because it reads energy patterns, but because of microscopic muscle movements in your arms and hands.

However, there is no doubt that most people can persuade a pendulum to swing in various ways – to and fro, left and right, and in circles. How do we do this? One explanation is *biofeedback.*

Biofeedback

Suppose you want the pendulum to swing in a clockwise circle. You may not consciously know how to make it do so, but you can unconsciously learn. You hold it there, and watch. You cannot see the tiny muscle movements in your hands, but their effects are greatly amplified by the pendulum. If your hand moves to the right, so will the bob, a short time later.

As you watch the bob moving you can unconsciously help it to move the way you want it to. If you want it to swing to the right, you will unconsciously amplify any tiny muscular movement that starts it moving that way. Your brain is only using the same system it uses to keep your body standing up or the bicycle moving where you want to go.

Naturally you can, if you wish, move your hand deliberately in a circle, and so move the pendulum. But the fact is that you can perform tiny movements unconsciously, and so bring about the same effect without meaning to do so.

So you, rather than the pendulum, have to be tuned in to get results. When you know that something is right, the biofeedback will reinforce the micromuscular twitches that give rise to clockwise circles of the bob.

If this is true, something interesting follows. The pendulum is a way of amplifying your unconscious ideas and feelings. This may be why the Abbé said not to *will* your pendulum. If you consciously try to force it you will only find out what you consciously knew already. More interesting is to use your pendulum to explore your deeper feelings. Do you really want to marry him? Asking your pendulum is not such a silly idea. If this theory is correct you will not learn whether you will live in happiness for ever and ever, but you might find out what you really think.

So is it true? Can the pendulum tap into unknown forces and tell you things you couldn't possibly have known, or is it just an amplifier of your own mind? You can do some simple experiments to find out.

Pendulum Experiments

A Simple Test

Take three identical coffee-jar lids, or yogurt pots, cups or saucers. Put them on the table in front of you and hide a coin under one of them.

Now take your pendulum, hold it over the first container, start it in the neutral position and then ask a simple question: 'Is the coin under this lid?'

Then move it to the next lid and ask it again, until you have done all three.

Does the pendulum locate the coin? If so, the pendulum is clearly not confused by the cover; its influence must work as though the cover were transparent.

How do you think this works? Can it sense the presence of the coin – or are *you* influencing the swing of the pendulum? Would you still succeed if you didn't know where the coin was?

A Harder Test

Get a friend to hide the coin under one of the three covers on the table, making sure you don't see where it is. Use your pendulum to pick out the right place. Be sure which is the correct cover – you have only one choice – and then take it off and look. Were you right? *Don't cheat, or say even to yourself, 'Oh, I really meant that one at the end.' Just make up your mind before you look.*

Even if you were right once, you might just have been lucky. If you want to turn this into a proper test you need to repeat it several times. We suggest trying it five times.

As long as you genuinely do not know in advance where the coin is, you can now find out whether the pendulum has real power, for if you are right four or five times in five guesses, there is a better than 95 per cent chance that you are not merely guessing.

What Does This Mean?

There are many other experiments you can do to find out whether the pendulum has real power for you.

Do you use your pendulum to determine whether food is good to eat? Some people are convinced this works – but then they can usually see the food in front of them. Ask a friend to hide some good food and some bad food under separate cups when you are out of the room and try it then.

You might even try this on a friend, hiding something truly disgusting under one of the cups – of course it mustn't be something that smells bad. A couple of dead flies might do nicely, with perhaps a sweet or a biscuit under the other.

To make this a significant test use three cups, with good food under only one of them. Do the test five times, getting someone else to mix up the food and the cups in between tests while you are out of the room.

Once again, if you can pick the good food four times out of five, you are unlikely to be just lucky; your pendulum is showing real power.

Finding Out your Star Sign

People often like to amaze their friends by correctly guessing their star sign. You may not be able to do this trick, but perhaps you and your pendulum together could get the right answer. On page 106 there is a chart to help you with this experiment.

First, hold your pendulum over the black spot and wait until it settles into its starting or zero position. Now think about your own star sign. Wait for a while, thinking all the time about your star sign. The pendulum may start swinging in circles or change direction but it should soon settle down. With luck it will end up swinging back and forth over one star sign. Did it get the right answer?

If it did, this could be because of the magical powers of the pendulum or because you knew the answer yourself. Time to try the test again with someone else.

Choose a friend or acquaintance whose birthday or star sign you do not know. Now repeat the test. Ask the pendulum 'Which is Sarah's star sign?' Wait until you are sure the pendulum has settled down to one sign and then write this guess down. Writing it down is important, because you might otherwise be tempted to change your guess when you hear the right answer. Once you have written it down you can ask Sarah for the right answer.

Did you get it right this time? If so, does this prove that the pendulum knew the answer?

Unfortunately the answer is still No. This may seem a little far-fetched, but it is still possible that Sarah's presence was giving the game away.

You may have played a party game like 'hunt the thimble' in which you are looking for something and all the people who know where it is shout 'warmer' as you get closer and 'colder' as you get further away. This way you can gradually home in on the right spot and find the thimble, sixpence or whatever.

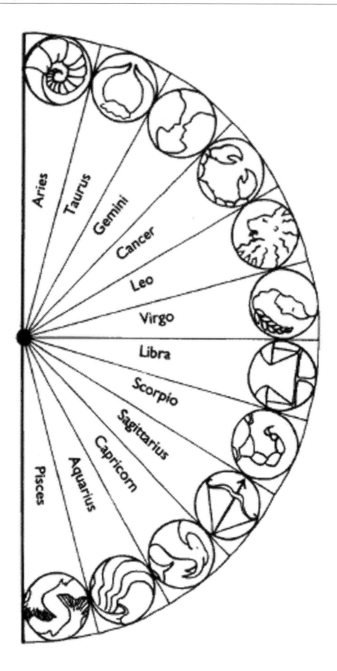

Figure 5.6: Start your pendulum swinging in the neutral position, to and fro over the black spot. Now ask, 'Which sun sign?' and wait for it to swing steadily over one of the signs.

This is easy when you have people shouting out the clues, but it is also possible to use the clues they give out unconsciously. For example, people often glance nervously towards the place where something is hidden. They also tense up when you approach the spot – and relax as you move away from it. You may not notice these changes consciously, but you could still be picking up on them unconsciously.

Magicians use a sophisticated version of this same idea to do tricks on large audiences. For example, they can track down a particular person or find a hidden object just by sensing the reactions of the audience. And people are amazed.

Even animals can do it. There was once a horse called 'Clever Hans' who appeared to be able to add and subtract. His trainer asked him questions such as 'What's three and five?' and he answered by pawing at the ground eight times, or whatever the answer was. He attracted enormous attention for his apparently miraculous powers. In the end a careful investigation showed that he was picking up the subtle changes of posture made by his trainer, who of course knew the right answers.

So it is just possible that you could be picking up clues like this from your friend, even if you don't consciously know her birthday or star sign.

To do a proper test you need to make sure that you cannot even see your friend, and that she cannot see the behaviour of the pendulum. There are several ways you can do this. Asking her to face the other way is easy but not completely foolproof. Better is to do the experiments at home on your own.

Ask your friend to send you the name of someone whose birthday you do not know. She might even like to send you a photo to look at while you use your pendulum. Once again, hold the pendulum over the starting point, think about the person and ask the question 'What star sign is this person?' When the pendulum has given you a satisfactory answer write it down.

Then check whether you were right. If you and your pendulum can succeed under these conditions, then you are doing well, for you cannot have subconsciously known the answer.

A Tough Test

Here is a good test you can do all by yourself without involving anyone else. You need a dice-shaker or plastic tumbler or beaker (not transparent), one die, and a saucer or book.

Put the die in the shaker or beaker. Put the book or saucer over the top. Shake the die, and turn the whole thing over so that the die lands on the book, but is still covered by the beaker.

Now your job is to find what is on top of the die before you take off the beaker and look. So ask 'Is it a 1?' and then 'Is it a 2?' and so on, until you are sure. Write down what you decide, and then look.

Try this twice. If you get your first two guesses right, there's a 97 per cent chance that you are not merely guessing. You can try as many times as you like. The table shows what chance (by percentage) you have of guessing the right number. For example, if you have four goes and get three right, there's only 1.5 per cent chance you were lucky – in other words a 98.5 per cent chance that you and your pendulum have power.

THE NUMBER ON THE DIE –

Number of trials	→	1	2	3	4	5
Number correct	0	83	69	58	48	40
	1	17	28	35	39	40
	2		3	7	12	16
	3			0.5	1.5	3
	4				0.1	0.3
	5					0.01

the percentage chance of getting it right

Scientists would say your result is significant if the percentage chance is less than 5 – so the shaded boxes at the bottom of the table are the ones you are aiming for – 2 out of 2, 3 out of 3, 3 or 4 out of 4; or 3 or more out of 5. But be sure to include *all* the results from one set of trials – these figures don't mean anything if you leave out one or two because they didn't work well.

I personally like to decide in advance on five trials. I set it up and go for five good guesses, partly because I feel that getting three right out of five doesn't seem too difficult – although I haven't succeeded yet!

Finding Lost Objects

Have you ever lost something in the garden or when out on a walk, or even in your own room, and wished you had a magic way to find it again? Some people claim that by using a pendulum they can find any lost object. Try this for yourself.

First you could try finding a coin under the carpet as you did with the rods or twigs (*see page* 80). Or get a friend to hide a small piece of jewellery somewhere in the room and see whether you can find it with your pendulum. By now you will be able to guess that, if your friend is in the room with you, you may be able to succeed at this task by picking up clues from her body movements or the way she is looking. So if you want to do this test properly make sure that no one in the room with you knows where the object is.

Even then it is difficult to make a perfect test because you might be able to see a slight bump under the carpet or notice the way it has been slightly disturbed. Another method of using the pendulum makes controlled tests easy, and that is map dowsing.

Map Dowsing

Some dowsers claim that they can locate things just by using a map. They usually use pendulums for this, rather than rods or twigs, because they say it is easier to be accurate with a pendulum.

Try this for yourself. To start with, make a map of your own room and see whether you can find an object in it. This makes a good test, because you can be as far away from the room as you like – so no peeping is possible. Also you can use a large and obvious object; it doesn't have to be hidden, because you won't be there to see it.

Choose an object that is meaningful for you. It doesn't matter what it is, as long as you can imagine that you would want to find it if it were lost.

Next ask a friend to place your object in the room you have chosen. When this is done, take your plan and hold your pendulum over it. Think about the object you have 'lost' and how much it means to you. Ask the pendulum to show you where it is. Now, slowly move the pendulum systematically over the plan and keep asking 'Is it here?', 'Is it here?' Your pendulum should give you the 'Yes' signal when it is over the right spot.

You may find that you can't easily tell precisely which point the pendulum indicates. This is when a bob with a pointer underneath helps. Some people prefer to use both hands, one to hold the pendulum, the other to point carefully at the map, either with a fingertip or with a pencil or some other pointer. Move your pointer systematically over the map, always asking 'Is it here?' In this way you should be able to narrow the position down to a small spot on the map.

Mark your guess on the plan and then go and have a look. Did you get it right?

Figure 5.7: To locate a position accurately on a map, scan the map systematically with one finger or a pencil, and hold the pendulum in the other.

There are still problems with this as a scientific test. Can you think of any?

One problem comes in deciding how close you have to be to the spot for it to count as right. Another is that you might simply guess where your friend has placed the object. Even if you tell her to pick an unusual place she might pick just the odd spot you were thinking of. Burglars can often find the things people try to hide, because they know that everyone puts their money under the mattress and their keys under the doormat. Surprisingly, many people still do this! Similarly, customs officers catch people who hide drugs in film tins or cosmetic jars.

To get round these problems you need a more systematic method, and you have to choose the spot randomly. One easy way to do this is to divide your plan up into squares – a bit like the grid on a town plan. Some dowsers like to use a grid on the map so they can go over each square asking the pendulum whether the object is there.

This method can be especially useful when you have to search large areas. For example, if you didn't even know which house an object was in, you could start with an A–Z plan of the city, divided into kilometre squares. Go over this systematically with your pendulum, asking 'Is it in this square? Is it in this square?'

When you have found the right square, take a larger scale map and reduce the search to squares 100 metres across. Next you can cut it down to a single house and finally start on the plan of one room.

An interesting option here is to dowse by postcodes. In the UK, the first letter or two give the city, the number gives the approximate area – so LS3 is an area west of the centre of Leeds. The final two digits narrow the search to a few houses. So in principle all you need is a list of the letters of the alphabet and the digits 0–9, and by running down the list with your pointer and asking the right questions you should quickly be able to get down to a few houses.

You don't need to do anything so complicated for this test, but you might like to use the grid method to divide your own room. We have drawn a plan of our living room to show one way of doing it. The rectangles are about 3x2 metres, but the exact size doesn't matter, as long as they cover the whole room.

Make a plan of your room, and draw a grid of six rectangles over it, numbering each rectangle, as we have. Then, *while you are in a different room,* get your friend to go into the room and throw a die to decide which square to put the object in; if she gets a five, for example, put it in the area covered on the plan by grid number five. Now she can bring you back the plan, and you can try your map dowsing. If you can find the correct rectangle the first two times you try, then your success is very unlikely to be just chance.

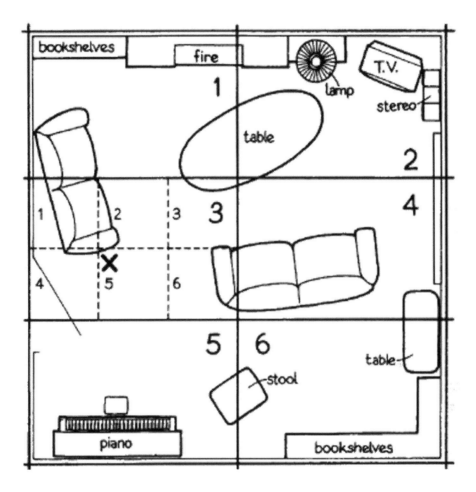

Figure 5.8: A plan of our living room divided into 36 squares. Get a friend to hide something you value in a room of your house. Can you find the exact square using only a plan and your pendulum?

A way to make an even more sensitive test is to use the small squares as well. Ask your friend to throw the die twice (when you are not looking, of course). She uses the first throw to decide which big rectangle to hide it in, and the second throw to decide which of the small ones within that large one. So, for example, if she threw 3 and 5 she would use the square marked X on our plan. If you can find the exact small rectangle with your pendulum using this test then there is only a 1 in 36 chance that it was just luck.

Were you successful? If you were, and you are sure you did not know in advance where the object was, then there must be something magical about the way the pendulum works. On the other hand, if you succeeded only in the tests when you knew the answer, then the powers of the pendulum probably lie within you.

6

Premonitions

Can anyone really see into the future? Wouldn't we all love to know what is going to happen – whether we are going to pass our exams, or fall in love (and with whom)? Should we take a particular job? Which horse is going to win the Grand National?

Sometimes these wishes are realized – but the results are not always good news.

The Hundred-to-One Winner

In London in 1967, Australian racing enthusiast George Cranmer woke on the morning of the Grand National with a big smile on his lips, for he had dreamt about watching the race and seeing the winner gallop past the post. Then he realized the dream had been so vivid he could clearly remember the colours worn by the jockey on the winning horse.

With his hands beginning to shake, he looked at the morning paper and discovered there was only one set of colours that matched those in his dream – light green with tartan cross belts, light blue sleeves and a tartan cap. Scarcely taking time for breakfast he went round to his bookmaker and placed a large bet on Foinavon.

The 1967 Grand National was a spectacular disaster. Two loose horses reached Beecher's Brook just before the rest of the field, and veered across the course. There was a tremendous pile-up. Horse after horse came to a shuddering stop, and jockey after jockey came crashing to the ground. John Buckingham, on the rank outsider Foinavon, was trailing so far behind that the chaos had almost cleared by the time he reached the fence; to the spectators Foinavon appeared to emerge like a dolphin from the sea of horses and riders on the ground.

Other jockeys remounted and gave chase, but Foinavon was so far ahead that no one could catch up, and he romped home at 100–1.

That was a dream well worth having. But in Cincinnati, 12 years later, a car mechanic would happily have done without his nightmare.

The DC10 Disaster

Early in the morning of Tuesday 15 May 1979, David Booth woke up crying and sobbing. His wife Pam calmed him down and asked what the problem was. He said he had had a dream about an air crash, and it was so sharp and real he felt dreadful.

Then he told her the details of his dream.

He was standing on a gravel road. There was a building on his right and a row of trees on his left, and as he looked up he saw a plane flying low overhead – a big silver passenger plane with *AMERICAN AIRLINES* painted on the side. The plane had three engines – one on each wing and one in the tail – and he noticed that it wasn't making much noise – much less noise than it should have been making for a plane that big and flying so low.

He looked to his right again and saw that the building seemed to be a school; it was a big building with a flat roof, and the pieces of paper taped up in the large windows looked like children's paintings. He looked back to his left at the row of trees, and as he looked up again he saw the huge plane roll slowly on to one wingtip and then plunge nose-down into the ground.

There was a great explosion and a huge ball of fire, and he knew that everyone in the plane was dead.

Again he shook uncontrollably, as the images flooded his mind.

'Don't worry, Dave,' Pam comforted him. 'It's only a dream!'

But he could not get the pictures out of his head, and all day he was haunted by the idea of the huge plane crashing and all the passengers and crew dying in the flames. He worked as an auto mechanic in a garage, but he did not work well that day, for his mind was elsewhere.

That night, apprehensively, he persuaded Pam to go to bed early. They went to sleep – and he had the same dream all over again. Exactly the same dream.

The third night he had the dream again. He could not change it. He still looked at the school, and at the trees, and then up just in time to see the plane begin to roll over.

He tried alcohol. He tried smoking. He sat up late and watched TV. He tried not going to bed at all. Nothing worked. Whatever he tried he had the same dream, for seven nights in a row. Not only was he increasingly distressed, and short of sleep; he also began to worry that this might be a premonition of a disaster still waiting to happen.

On the eighth day, a Wednesday, he phoned American Airlines and tried to tell them about the dream, but they refused to take any action and advised him to go to a psychiatrist. In despair he called Cincinnati Airport, and finally spoke to the Federal Aviation Administration, who control all non-military flights in the United States.

FAA officer Paul Williams took the story seriously, and realized that if this were an event in the future he might be able to prevent it. On Thursday 24 May he questioned Booth on the phone for 45 minutes, trying to extract all the available details. Could David see the registration letters on the plane? Was there a sign on the school, or on the road? Were there any other landmarks that might help to pinpoint the place? Over and over the story he went, trying to establish where it might have happened – or where it might be going to happen.

The following day, Friday 25 May, Paul Williams was driving home after work when he heard on his car radio news of a dreadful air crash in Chicago. An *American Airlines* DC10 three-engined jet had crashed immediately after take-off, and all 273 passengers and crew had died in the explosion and fire that followed. It was the worst aviation disaster in American history.

Paul Williams said the radio report sounded like a replay of what David Booth had told him the day before.

The cause of the crash was established much later. Following faulty maintenance procedures, an engine had come loose from the wing as the pilot called for maximum power on take-off. The entire engine had swung down from the wing and then up over the top of it, ripping away all the control cables as it fell. As the aircraft left the ground the pilot was left not only with one less engine than he expected, but also with no flaps or other controls in one wing. As a result, the stricken aircraft performed a startling and unique manoeuvre – it rolled on to one wingtip and plunged downwards.

Paul Williams said, 'Maybe it was just a coincidence, but the airline was exactly right, and the type of aircraft was the same. Perhaps the most remarkable coincidence of the whole thing was the similarity of the manoeuvre the plane made. It's a very unusual manoeuvre for a plane to make before crashing. Most of them crash with their wings horizontal; they run into some obstruction, or there is a mid-air collision. But the manoeuvre David described was very unusual. As a matter of fact, it's the only one I ever heard of in a plane that size!'

Television Previews?

Premonitions come to people in all sorts of different ways, sometimes even on television. One remarkable example seems to have happened in Grimsby, a fishing port on the east coast of England, on 1 June 1974.

Lesley Brennan was sitting at home watching the Saturday morning film on television when, she says, the story was interrupted by a newsflash. There were no pictures, just the word NEWSFLASH and a man's voice saying that there had been an explosion and fire at Flixborough, near Grimsby. There was some technical information that she did not understand, and some news about how many people had been killed and injured.

She was slightly interested, because it was a local story, but she wanted the newsflash to be over soon so that she could watch the rest of the film.

Two friends of hers, Janice and Peter East, came to lunch and Lesley told them about the newsflash; they were concerned about the tragic loss of life.

That evening they were all together when the television news came on. The lead story was the disaster at Flixborough, as they expected. What they did not expect was for the reporter to say that the explosion had happened at about 5 p.m. that day. They assumed the local TV company had made a mistake. But when they saw the papers next morning they discovered the explosion had frozen all the clocks in the plant at 4.53 p.m.

Janice and Peter were astounded. 'But you told us about that at lunch-time!'

Somehow, Lesley Brennan seems to have become aware of the Flixborough disaster five hours before it happened.

In a curiously similar incident, Mike Veshecco saw words on the screen in the middle of the TV news. They said something like STABBING IN CITY or LOCAL MAN STABBED, and he thought it was a teaser for a news item after the ads – but there was no such item. Mike was interested because he was district attorney in Erie County, Pennsylvania, and if there had been a stabbing he would probably be called out to the scene of the crime.

Both he and his wife said they saw the newsflash, and so by chance did county detective John Ross and his wife, at their home a few miles away. John also expected to be called out.

But no phone calls came, and in the morning Mike Veshecco went in early to the office to find out what had gone wrong with the communications. What he discovered was much more bizarre.

There had indeed been a stabbing in the city, and a man was dead – but the body had not been found until 7.30 a.m., and the murder turned out to have taken place at about 3 a.m.; so when Mike and John saw the STABBING newsflash, the victim was still alive...

Can We See the Future?

In our ordinary everyday lives, there is only one time – the present. But there has been past time. We have evidence of it. The fact that you are reading this book now means that we must have written it in the past – and it has been edited and printed and sold or loaned to you. But we have no evidence of the future. At any one time we cannot even be sure that there is going to be any future.

There are many equations in mathematics and physics that work just as well backwards as forwards. Sometimes we can use this to our advantage. For example, suppose you are shown a piece of rope tied in a beautiful knot and you want to know how it was done; one way to find out is to untie it slowly and carefully, and then reverse the process and tie it up again. You will then produce the same knot, by a process of reversal.

But we can't do this in most areas of life. We cannot retrace the past exactly, nor live in the future – we can only exist in the present.

Weather forecasters and stock-brokers spend their lives trying (with the help of huge computers) to predict what will happen tomorrow and the next day. Their success is limited, and when they are successful this is the result of extrapolating from the past rather than of looking directly into the future. So, if some people really do get glimpses of tomorrow, then they have to be using a paranormal process.

The first thing to establish is whether some people really do get glimpses of the future. I remember as a teenager I often used to wake in the morning with a feeling of 'impending doom', as I described it at the time. I felt that something terrible was going to happen. This feeling might come over me once a week or so. Now, on most of those days nothing terrible did happen; the feeling went away and life carried on as usual. But just occasionally I missed the bus, or was late for class, or I cut myself. Then I might easily have decided, with hindsight, that I had somehow 'known' something bad was going to happen, forgetting about all the times that I'd had the 'impending doom' feeling and nothing whatsoever bad had happened.

Dreams often seem to come true, but the same problem applies. Suppose you dream about an air crash, and the next day there is an air crash that matches your recollection of your dream. You might be astonished, but unless you have written down the details of your dream before you hear of the real event, you cannot tell how good the match is, because your brain will tend to confuse your dream with the real event.

Also, we dream many times every night and each dream includes countless images. When something odd happens during the day it is quite likely to match up with something from a dream and, indeed, to jog our memory of that dream. In this way lots of apparent matches can be found. But are they premonitions? There is only one way to find out to write down all such feelings or dreams at the time (or very soon afterwards), and see whether the foretold events happen.

One good way of organizing this is to set up your own 'premonitions bureau', simply to record premonitions. If you do this you will be following in the footsteps of the first British Premonitions Bureau, set up in 1967.

The School that Died

One of the most tragic dreams we know came to nine-year-old Eryl Mai Jones in a valley in South Wales. She woke on the morning of 20 October 1966 and said to her mother, 'You must listen to my dream. I dreamed I went to school and there was no school there. Something black had come down all over it.' The next morning a huge heap of coal waste, loosened by prolonged rain, slipped down the side of the valley in Aberfan and swallowed the Pantglas Junior School, killing 28 adults and 116 children, including Eryl Mai Jones.

Dr Barker, a consultant psychiatrist, visited Aberfan the following day and was appalled by the suffering he found there. It occurred to him that there might have been people throughout Britain who had experienced some forewarning of the disaster, and he decided to take this opportunity to investigate premonitions.

He contacted Peter Fairley, Science Correspondent of the London *Evening Standard,* who launched an appeal for cases. Dr Barker received 76 letters, and investigated 60 of them further. Many of the 'premonitions' turned out to be extremely vague and barely related to the events at Aberfan, and very few were written down *before* the tragedy. However, two weeks before the landslide one woman dreamed of 'screaming children and creeping black substance'; this was confirmed by her husband. Another had a 'spirit message' about 100 children being engulfed in black mud, and this was confirmed by a witness.

I cannot help wondering whether or not these people were truly seeing into the future. If they were, perhaps someone could have prevented the tragedy. If not, the reality may be that people are always imagining and dreaming about such things, and the timing was no more than a coincidence. How can we find out?

Premonitions Bureau

Peter Fairley's Premonitions Bureau began its collecting by inviting people to write in or telephone; the Bureau then simply listed the premonition with a date and time stamp, and waited to see what happened.

In the first year they were sent more than 1,000 premonitions, many of which were surprisingly accurate, although none sufficiently detailed to help avert a tragedy. A few 'stars' emerged – people who had several 'hits'. But when Fairley asked them to come in for interviews, they seemed to lose their ability to predict. His view was that premonitions come spontaneously, and that to think about the future and try for premonitions is to destroy the gift.

You could try your own investigation into premonitions, by setting up a Bureau along the same lines. This needs quite a bit of time and effort, but the results could be fascinating. In any case, setting it up should bring you into contact with some interesting people!

Setting Up your Own Premonitions Bureau

You need two things to set up a Premonitions Bureau:

1. a source of lots of premonitions
2. a way of classifying and analysing them

Collecting the Premonitions

There are many ways to get hold of premonitions. You might advertise through newspapers, radio, or television. You might go around asking people in the street, or try to find local psychics who claim to have frequent premonitions. If you have been keeping a dream diary (as suggested in Chapter 3), you might use your own dreams as a source of premonitions, or set up a group who will all look out for precognitive dreams and send them in. One easy way to do it is if you have access to a school or college or company magazine; we will use that as our example here.

You need an advertisement that will catch people's eye and make them want to take part in your project; you could get it into the magazine or a local paper, and also pin it up on several notice boards. You might write an article for the magazine about precognition – tell one of the stories we have given here, or give examples you have come across. You might find there is a television programme that includes such stories and use that as a starting point. However you do it, once people are interested in the question of premonitions you can ask them to help you in a scientific project to find out whether it is all true or not.

The advert might run something like this:

Have you ever had a premonition?
Frustrated because no one took you seriously?
Then join our **Premonitions Bureau.**

What to Do

- Send in a brief account of what you think is going to happen.
- State when and how you had the premonition (e.g. a vision or dream).
- Send your premonition to us as soon as you can and **definitely before the event comes true.** It is no use to send your account after the event. We must have it recorded in our files before the event occurs.
- Send it to ......

There are several things to note about this advertisement – and you may think of better ways of setting it out so that it meets all the necessary criteria.

First, it must catch people's eye.

Second, you must persuade them to keep their stories brief. You will realize how important this is as soon as you get some premonitions coming in. Many people think their own dreams are so exciting that they write pages and pages about them. What you want is just the nub of the story – just that one odd event that might prove to come true. So try to persuade people to give you just that and no more.

Third, you need to emphasize the importance of logging the premonitions before the event comes true. It is absolutely no use to you to have a whole pile of letters about premonitions that have already come true. It misses the whole point of having a Premonitions Bureau. People might have mis-remembered the events, or recalled their dreams as more similar to the events than they really were. They might even have made them all up. So make this absolutely clear. *You will have* to *throw away any accounts you get of events that have already happened.*

Finally, you need to consider how people are to send their material to you. You might rely on the ordinary post. The problem here is that it takes at least a day, and often more, for a letter to arrive – and in the mean time the event might have happened. It would be awful to receive a stunning pre-cognition of a plane crash in Siberia in the post the morning *after* you watched the crash on television. You would have to throw it away, because there would be a chance that a fluke had got the letter to you very quickly or that the person had faked the postmark!

If you are working within a college, school or other organi-zation you may be able to provide a special posting box into which people could put their accounts as soon as they have written them. You could lock it so that no one else can get at the contents, and empty it at regular intervals.

Or you might use a fax machine. This has the advantage that people can send in their accounts from anywhere, they arrive almost immediately, and the fax machine records the time on the fax itself, but in this case you must make sure you collect the faxes at regular intervals and don't allow them to lie around. Someone might just hear about an unusual event and sneak in with a faked fax to add to the pile. You would feel pretty silly if you got tricked this way.

However you collect them, you must lock them away so that no one can slip in fake premonitions long after the event has happened. Only you must be able to get at the collection.

Once you have started collecting the accounts you need to log them in.

Logging the Premonitions

You need to take logging seriously, to make sure you know exactly when every premonition is received by your Bureau. The person who has the premonition ought to write the time and date on it, but you also need to record the time and date on which you receive it. You might get a special stamp to do this, or simply write the time and date on each one, but try to make it hard for anyone to cheat later on.

For example, you might write the time and date on each one in bright red indelible ink; but if people see what you are doing they might try to copy it – and sneak in a 'premonition' of something that has already happened with an earlier date written on it in bright red.

You might want to sign your own name next to the red mark to make it difficult for someone else to fake it, but in any case your best weapon against fraud is probably secrecy. If no one but you knows how you log the premonitions, and they are all kept locked safely way, then it will hard for the cheat to succeed.

You may think this sounds a little paranoid – trying to stop cheating before you have any evidence that there are any cheats. But the history of psychical research is littered with experiments ruined by cheats, and others that nobody takes seriously because someone *could* have cheated. If you do get any stunning premonitions then you will have to prove to other people's satisfaction that they could not have been tricks. So doing it properly really is worth while.

Classifying the Premonitions

Your job will be easier if you classify each premonition as soon as you get it. For example, you might follow the original Bureau in dividing the accounts into those concerning:

> air and space
> road, rail and sea
> royal family
> personalities
> politics, war and riots
> economy
> crime
> sport
> natural disasters
> explosions, fire and collapse of buildings
> miscellaneous.

You might also like to divide them into categories of how they came about – such as dreams, 'feelings', visions, or spirit messages.

Analysing the Results

This the hardest part of running your Bureau. You can choose simple analysis, or something more complex. Here are a few ideas you might try.

Collecting Hits

This is the simplest method. Just watch to see whether any of the premonitions you have collected come true, and check that they were logged and dated *before* the event.

If you are lucky you may have one or two premonitions that seem so unlikely to have happened by chance that you are really impressed. You can then be sure that the dream or vision or whatever really did happen in advance of the event. Suppose, for example, George Cranmer had written down his dream of the winning horse and had sent it in to your Bureau two hours before the race – you would have a much more impressive case than we have today.

There are problems with this, however. Let us suppose that you do get an impressive case, such as someone who predicts a train crash and sends you an account of the incident three days before it happens. You may be very impressed and quite convinced that this is really precognition. But how good a match was it? Did the person see the right kind of train? Did he or she even specify what sort of train it was? Did he or she say whether it was at night or in the day, or whether anyone was killed or not? Does the crash of a goods train near a small village at night count as confirmation of a dream in which 87 people are killed in a passenger train during the London rush hour?

In other words, when does a premonition count as a hit? Another simple method avoids this problem.

Looking for Patterns

Once you have collected enough premonitions you can look to see whether they follow any unusual or surprising patterns. For example, you could make a table or a graph to show the number of plane-crash premonitions that come in every month. Then you will be able to notice if there is a sudden increase in the number of plane-crash reports – or a sudden flood of stories about a death in the royal family.

If the occurrence of 'premonitions' is just chance, the event is unlikely to happen in reality – but if the premonitions are real it ought to come quick on the heels of your observed increase in reports.

Alternatively you could take a surprising event and look backwards, to see whether any of your reports could have been premonitions of it. For example, let us suppose that during the time you are running your Bureau there is an earthquake in Scotland – an extremely unlikely event. Now you might look back and see whether there are any references to earthquakes or Scotland. If you find some, you need to look at the patterns again.

You might plot out the number of references to Scotland or earthquakes over the whole time of your Bureau's operation. If all the references you have are evenly spread out over the weeks or months, then they are probably all down to chance – but if they all came in just before the time of the event then they are more likely to be genuine premonitions.

Scoring the Premonitions

Much more complicated systems are possible. In his Bureau, Peter Fairley gave each premonition a score of between 0 and 15. First he gave them up to 5 points for the unusualness of the predicted event. So, for example, a dream of a plane crash or a fire might score only 2 or 3 because these things happen relatively often, but a dream about the Queen coming to your town on an elephant would definitely score 5.

Then Mr Fairley gave up to five points for the level of detail. For example, you might give only 1 to a premonition of a fire in a ship, but 5 if the name of the ship were given or the exact markings on its hull were described. Finally, Fairley gave up to 5 for the precision of timing. So, a premonition that Madonna gets married might get a 0, but that she was to get married on 22 September at 6.15 p.m. would score 5.

Next you might award a score for accuracy. For example, if the Queen came to a nearby town in a normal car you might give a score of 1, but if she really turned up on an elephant you would give the maximum score. If you decide to use a scoring system like this you will have to plan your system carefully in advance, and then score every premonition for detail as soon as it comes in. Later you can score it for how nearly it comes true.

The main problem with any system like this is that it is highly subjective, and you will probably find it hard to decide on what scores to give. The advantage is that you can place greater weight on the most specific premonitions, and compare different people's premonitions to see how well they do. Like Peter Fairley, you will probably find that some people do better than others and you can now give them a score. But does this mean the high scorers are really psychic?

They could just be lucky. Inevitably some people do have runs of good and bad luck – but this soon runs out and they go back to being like everyone else. This applies to lots of things in life – such as catching that bus that seems to come at completely unpredictable times every morning. Some days you step out of the house – and it is just coming down the street. You might even have a whole week when this happens every day, and you begin to think you have the gift of precognition and know when the bus is coming. By chance there will always be runs of good and bad luck. The difference is that, if you really have psychic powers, your success ought to continue, but if it is just chance someone else will start having the good luck next week.

It's the same with premonitions. Maybe there really are people who can predict the future, and maybe it is all just chance. With a properly organized Premonitions Bureau you should be able to find out for yourself.

Finding the Psychics

When you have calculated the scores for each person you might find that Ms X has the highest score so far, and Mr Y the second highest, with everyone else trailing behind.

You might then make your own prediction: If Ms X and Mr Y are psychic, then they should carry on getting higher scores. However, if they just happen to have been having a run of good luck, then they are no more likely than anyone else to get good scores next time. Indeed, by the law of averages, or 'regression to the mean', anyone with extreme scores in one month is likely to get more average scores next time. So watch your 'star performers' over a few months, and see how they get on.

Ideally you should specify in advance how long you will give them. This will prevent you from stopping your experiment just when one or other of them has another bit of luck. So, for example, you might give it exactly six months and at the end of that time add up everyone's scores, take an average score and see whether Ms X and Mr Y have done better than average for almost all the time.

Predicting the Next Disaster

In the end, if there really are premonitions it ought to be possible to predict a future disaster, and even perhaps avoid it – but somehow this never seems to happen.

One sceptical magazine has taken the trouble, each year, to collect up all the predictions made by famous psychics for that year. By the end of the year most people have forgotten what the predictions were – but not the sceptics. And what they have found is a long list of mundane 'predictions' – of war, disaster, accidents and gossip; some of which came true and some not. What they have never found is truly surprising predictions that came true.

The fall of the Berlin wall in November 1989 was a momentous event occasioning festivities, reunions and excitement all over the world. But it was not clearly foretold by psychics.

The breakdown of the Soviet Union brought the Cold War to an end, dramatically reduced people's fear of nuclear warfare and changed the world for ever. That too was not predicted.

Yet tales of premonitions keep on coming. Why? Coincidence and wishful thinking? With your Premonitions Bureau you can help to investigate this persistent mystery.

Were the Stories True?

No doubt George Cranmer did win money on Foinavon in the Grand National, but his story of a dream – which he told to Peter Fairley – is unsubstantiated. We have no evidence that he wrote anything about it when he woke up. He may merely have been lucky, and afterwards embroidered the tale.

David Booth's story of the dream of an air crash is much harder to explain. David was clear and definite about what he had seen in the dream, and his wife remembers the occasion well. What makes his story so intriguing is the evidence of Paul Williams. It is possible that Williams and Booth were in league, and agreed to stick to the same fabricated story – but that seems most unlikely. If Williams is telling the truth, which seems to be the case, then Booth's story is extremely hard to explain. Perhaps it was just a coincidence – but that does seem highly improbable.

A Cautionary Tale

On 19 February 1979, Richard Newton of Rockport, Massachusetts, predicted an air crash in writing and on ▶

television. He said that on 11 March a plane with a red logo on the tail would crash just outside a major city in the northern hemisphere, and that 46 people would be killed.

On 14 March a Royal Jordanian Airlines jet (with a red logo on the tail) crashed just outside Doha in the Persian Gulf, and 45 people died.

Was he psychic? Did he have a premonition? No; he did it all by statistics. He read books about air crashes, and discovered that they almost always happen on take-off or landing – that is near airports, which are always just outside large cities. The great majority of the large cities with airports are in the northern hemisphere. Of all the airlines in service in 1979, more than half had some red in the logos on their tails.

The average number of people killed in all the air crashes in the previous 23 years was 46, which was why he guessed that number. And finally he examined the number of crashes in each week of the year, and found that the most dangerous month of the year seemed to be March, and that the most dangerous week seemed to be the second week in March – the Ides of March, as Julius Caesar would have called them!

So he made his prediction of what seemed most likely, based on the history of air crashes, and he was almost exactly right.

What about the story of Lesley Brennan and Flixborough? We have spoken to Lesley Brennan, and to Peter East. Unless they are both mistaken, Lesley seems to have seen and said something about a disaster at Flixborough some time before it happened. However, the local television station had no record of having put out a newsflash.

▶

What about Mike Veshecco and John Ross? Do you think both they and their wives were making the whole thing up? Surely if that were the case they would have invented a more dramatic incident, and got their stories more precisely organized.

How might a premonitions bureau have helped in each case?

7

Psychokinesis

In November 1973 television audiences in the UK were agog at the exploits of a young Israeli called Uri Geller. Lean, saturnine and good-looking, Geller appeared on the *David Dimbleby Talk-in* claiming that he could bend forks and spoons and keys using only the power of his mind. Lo and behold, as millions watched the slightly wobbly close-up shots, a fork did indeed bend and break – the end fell right off. Fellow guests Professor John Taylor and Dr Lyall Watson could scarcely believe their eyes.

Geller seemed merely to hold the fork gently in one hand, and stroke the top of the handle with the tips of his fingers, while saying 'Yes, yes, it's becoming like plastic...', and the fork did seem to turn as soft as butter in his hands. The prongs flapped soggily to and fro, and then as he said 'It's breaking!' the end collapsed and fell off.

After another fork had broken Geller said, with apparent surprise, 'And there's no heat at all!'

Uri Geller said the fork was broken by mind-power; that this was simply one example of mind over matter.

Geller went on to claim he could make clocks and watches which had stopped years before start going again. The power of the mind was enough, he said, to reactivate machinery.

He proceeded, during the programme, to start at least one watch – and to stop at least one other.

What is more, all over the country people said they found spoons and forks and keys that were bent, and clocks and watches that had started up after being stopped for many years. His amazing power must have travelled with the TV signal, they said. Geller said he thought it more likely that he simply acted as a trigger, and released in other people powers they did not know they had. Suddenly, up and down the nation children found that they too could bend spoons, and the kitchen table drawers of Britain gradually filled with contorted cutlery...

Several scientists, including Professor John Taylor from King's College London, said they could detect no trickery. They endorsed Geller's claims and said that these strange events deserved to be subjected to thorough scientific investigation.

Uri Geller had certainly unleashed a novel craze on the nation.

Psychokinesis

This apparently new phenomenon, startling the first time you see it, is called *psychokinesis* (PK). PK originally meant 'motion caused by the mind', but its definition was extended to include all physical influencing of objects by mind-power alone. It has taken over from the older term 'telekinesis', which means moving objects from a distance.

Geller did not invent PK; reports of such events have been around at least since Darwin's time. Just as we would all love to be able to communicate with our minds, so we would also like to have the mind-power to move inanimate objects. Over the course of human history many people have claimed they could do this. The question is, did they imagine it, or fool onlookers, or could they really bring about mind-powered movement?

In 1956, New Zealander Dr Rolf Alexander claimed he could persuade clouds to break up merely by staring at them and exerting his will-power.

An impressive exponent of PK was Mrs Nelya Mikhailova, from Leningrad, also known as Madame Kulagina. She was filmed in the 1960s moving various objects on a table in front of her without touching them with her hands. She made a metal rod roll to and fro, and a compass needle swing violently round when she leaned over it.

A part-time lift-operator from near Chicago, Ted Serius (sometimes also known as Ted Serios), claimed he could 'think' images directly on to photographic film, and produced, on an instant camera inside a television studio in Denver, pictures of such famous buildings as the Eiffel Tower.

In Rolla, Missouri, W. E. Cox and Dr J. T. Richards sealed a number of curious objects in an upturned fish-tank, which was left in Cox's garage. While it was sealed up and unattended, they said, strange events happened inside: balloons inflated, wool strands became plaited, and words were written on paper. They even captured some of these events on 8-mm film!

Scientific Research

The phenomena of PK seem so extraordinary that several scientists have set up extensive research programmes to try and work out how the mind could possibly perform such feats. After all, to bend a spoon, or a key, requires considerable force and considerable energy. How can the mind exert force? There is no simple scientific mechanism.

The first scientist to attempt to investigate PK rigorously was J. B. Rhine at Duke University in North Carolina in the 1930s. Rhine had already been investigating ESP for some years (see *page* 8) when he met a gambler who claimed he could use will-power to influence the fall of dice on the gaming tables. Rhine did some investigating on his own, and became convinced that he could do so too. Accordingly he began serious investigations.

Rhine tried various sizes of dice, and various types of people – in one experiment he pitted divinity students against gamblers, both sides putting their faith to the test! He invented dice-throwing machines to eliminate human bias, and tested the effects of plying the participants with alcohol and caffeine. His results, published during the Second World War, were treated with scepticism by the scientific establishment.

Dr Helmut Schmidt, at the Mind Science Foundation in San Antonio, Texas, was the pioneer of 'electronic coin-tossing'. He used the natural radioactive decay of a specimen of strontium-90 to power a random-number generator and so to produce equal numbers of + and - signals. Tests without a subject showed that + and - were equally likely to occur.

Subjects would sit in front of a display of nine light bulbs arranged in a circle, only one of them lit. When + came up, the lit bulb moved clockwise; when - came up, it moved anti-clockwise. Subjects were asked to concentrate on the bulbs. Sometimes they were asked to try to move the light clockwise around the circle, and sometimes anti-clockwise. Naturally, the subjects did not understand all the clever electronics inside the machine, but the theory was that this did not matter. It was enough that they should see the lights moving and *desire* the light to go in one direction or the other.

The curious result was that many of them seemed to have some ability to move the light the wrong way – opposite to the way they were trying for. Although this appears to be a failure, some parapsychologists argue that it is just as impressive, and shows a direct effect of the mind on subatomic processes – something that would potentially challenge the very foundations of physics.

Geller's 1973 appearance started the scientific ball rolling again in Britain. Professor John Hasted of Birkbeck College, London University found after Geller's performances that some teenagers could produce amazing 'paperclip scrunches'. These were twisted, convoluted tangles of paperclips all squeezed and twisted together. To make them would seem to have required strong fingers and several pairs of pliers. But what made them extraordinary was that each scrunch was produced inside a delicate glass bulb with only one tiny hole. To feed in a few straight paperclips seemed possible, but to twist and scrunch them together seemed utterly impossible.

His subjects claimed they did it merely by the power of thought – although curiously Hasted never witnessed any of the scrunches actually being done.

Hasted also devised complex metal-bending tasks, in which the slightest movement of the metal would be measured by strain gauges. He sat his subjects in Faraday cages to isolate them from external sources of radiation. Meanwhile, John Taylor and others tried to pin down Geller's powers.

In 1979, volunteers were invited to go for detailed investigation to the McDonnell parapsychology laboratory at Washington University in the US – popularly known as the MacLab. And this was where James Randi stepped into the picture.

Project Alpha

James (the Amazing) Randi is a magician who has spent decades entertaining the American public with magical tricks and feats of prestidigitation. He has long been sceptical of claims for paranormal powers, and was particularly doubtful about Uri Geller.

Randi claimed he could bend spoons, 'repair' watches and reproduce all Geller's other phenomena simply by trickery and sleight of hand. Therefore, he said, Geller was just a magician, not psychic at all. He needed no special powers. However, Randi was reluctant to show all his tricks in slow motion, since his career as a magician depended on them.

When the new MacLab asked for volunteers, however, he saw his chance. Steve Shaw and Mike Edwards were aspiring magicians who had met Randi earlier. They volunteered themselves as subjects for the MacLab, where they claimed they had been struck by lightning as children and since then had found they could do amazing things.

They were taken on as subjects, and astonished the scientists by their extraordinary feats. For example, one of them (when no one else was around) put a cheap digital watch into a microwave oven for a minute, which half-melted the plastic case. He then put it on, under his shirt cuff, and later in the middle of an experiment claimed he suddenly felt a tingling in his wrist. He glanced at the watch and shouted out 'WOW!! Look what happened to my watch!'

Another trick was to set up an 'experiment' and fail, and then ask to look at the videotape – for everything they did was taped. From the tape Steve and Mike could see exactly how much they could get away with. When Mike noticed that one of the cameramen was particularly good at close-ups of his hands, he would set up a pre-bent spoon for a fake PK experiment and then ask for that cameraman to come and act as his assistant – so that he could not operate the camera and catch Mike on tape in the act of sleight of hand. Then Mike knew he could work the trick of pretending to bend the spoon.

When they needed to distract the observers they would ask for a glass of hot water, knowing that this would take someone out of the room for several minutes, giving them a chance for a bit more trickery.

Randi told both Steve and Mike to tell the truth – never to say they were doing things by mind-power and at once to confess if they were accused of being magicians. But apparently no one suspected a thing; the truth was only revealed to the embarrassed scientists by Randi at a press conference. Mike and Steve's 'feats' had all been faked.

PK or no PK – That is the Question!

Telepathy is intriguing because the best stories are 'spontaneous' – they are anecdotes about amazing events that have happened when no one was expecting them. Likewise, premonitions seem to be beyond the control of the seer. PK is rather different. PK seems to happen mainly when someone *wants* it to – although you do hear about people who can't wear watches because they go haywire, and people who cause photocopying machines to cry 'TILT. Maybe every time a picture falls off the wall – or a milk bottle jumps out of the fridge – that is spontaneous PK in action. Indeed, while I was sitting minding my own business in the bathroom last week, a glued-on hook fell off the wall in the shower with a terrible clatter. Was that PK too?

According to some people, the entire paranormal world is driven by PK. Premonitions are simply PK in action. You predict the dice will come up double-6 next time, but you are really influencing it by PK. Likewise, telepathy could be simply PK. You think of the ace of spades, and force that picture into your partner's mind by the power of your own. Deal a pack of cards and name each one before you turn it face-up? Easy! By the power of your mind you have simply rearranged the cards so that they come up in the order you have already chosen.

But what about those plane crashes? Could you really believe that people who seem to predict a disaster are actually *creating* it by their own thoughts? Could little Eryl Mai Jones and her friends have *created* the coal slip at Aberfan? That thought is both deeply disturbing and rather unlikely.

If PK exists at all, its limits are unclear. The term *poltergeist* actually means 'noisy spirit', but some people think that poltergeists have nothing to do with the dead. The effects are, according to one theory, caused by the PK powers of the focus-person. This might be a disturbed teenager whose bottled-up frustrations come out in uncontrolled bursts of PK, or a lonely child whose fantasies 'spill out' into paranormal powers. This is why some modern parapsychologists refer to poltergeists as RSPK, or *recurrent spontaneous psychokinesis.*

Nevertheless, even if it doesn't exist PK must be powerful stuff, for in a sense it brought together the authors of this book! Adam Hart-Davis first met Susan Blackmore when he filmed her baby daughter (then nearly 2 years old) sitting in front of a computer, working on an extension of the Schmidt experiments. In the computer was a programme that produced on the screen either just a dull grey pattern with a hissing sound or a smiling face and a nursery-rhyme tune. How often the face and tune appeared was controlled by a random-number generator. When left to its own devices, the face appeared say six times a minute. The theory was that if Emily liked the face – which she clearly did – then by PK she might be able to influence the random-number generator to put the face on the screen more often than would be expected by chance.

Figure 7.1 : Baby PK. The computer is controlled by a random-number generator. Can the baby influence it to produce the tune and face more often?

Clearly the baby could not understand the mechanism by which she could influence the machine, but the PK experts claimed this did not matter. All that mattered was that she wanted one particular outcome, and if she wanted it enough she could make it happen. (Which is interesting, because it implies that if you *really* want someone to fall in love with you – or if you *really* want time to jump on 10 minutes – you should be able to bring it about. But perhaps we don't all have enough belief in our psychic powers.)

In the end Emily did better than she should have done just by chance. But later Susan discovered problems in the random-number generator – that it wasn't completely random after all. The researcher who made it claimed it was functioning perfectly – but perhaps we shall never know for sure. Once again, real proof of PK powers has evaded us.

So the whole field of PK is riddled with claim and counter-claim, with accusations of errors, fraud and cheating. The question is, does it exist at all? We literally cannot answer that question – but you can try to find an answer for yourself, by experimentation.

Simple Tests

Can you make the traffic lights change to green as you approach? Or can you make automatic doors open before you get within the range of the detector? Some people believe they can affect street lamps – for example make them flicker and go out – whenever they walk by. This is a good one to test, and there is even a research project in London called SLIDE – or Street Lamp Interference Data Exchange.

For a proper test you can't just watch for lamps to go out as you pass by. After all, they might have been on the blink anyway. But you can do tests on them. Observe a particular lamp from a good distance for a measured length of time – say 5 minutes – and count how many times (if at all) it flickers or goes out. Then spend another 5 minutes walking up and down underneath it. Is it really affected by your presence?

You might like to work out a similar test to find out whether you or your friends can influence the clouds. Can you really clear up the weather for that special picnic – or for Wimbledon – or is it just wishful thinking?

Several famous psychics have claimed they can make a compass needle move by the power of their minds, even though it should always point north. If you place a compass on a flat surface and make sure that there are no magnets nearby, it should settle down and remain quite still (remember there are powerful magnets in the speakers of your radio and stereo or CD player). Now, can you 'will' it to move one way or the other?

Have a Spoon-Bending Party

Why not try collective PK in a way that could be more fun than a serious scientific test? Invite your friends to come to a party, each bringing a spoon and fork. The idea is for many people all to try to bend spoons at the same time. There are two good reasons for this. First, PK is supposed to be collective – if many people want some outcome, it is apparently more likely to happen than if only one person wants it. Secondly, they say that if you lark about and have fun, psychic things become enabled – or at least more probable.

At a spoon-bending party we went to in California, 20 people sat around in the living room, each holding up a spoon or fork in one hand. They chatted and joked, and then came the call for collective effort. Everyone held their objects up in front of their faces and focused on them. The host called out, loudly, 'Come on, all together now, *bend, bend,* BEND!' The shout was so loud it must have startled the neighbours beyond the swimming pool. Everyone had a lot of fun, and by the end of the party the table was covered with twisted spoons and forks. We did not actually see any single bend happen spontaneously – but then we did not see anyone cheating either; so perhaps collective PK was working that night. Why don't you try it, too – but don't forget to get your guests to bend their *own* spoons, or you may have no straight ones left for your breakfast!

Animal PK

Can you persuade woodlice, by the power of your mind, to move into one half of a box?

For this test you will need an Assistant, a watch that shows seconds, and some woodlice. The test works better with an odd number of woodlice; we reckon seven or nine, but one, three, five or eleven will do. Their favourite places are in wood-piles, but you should be able to find woodlice under loose stones or flowerpots in the garden or in a park.

Collect them in a small box – such as a matchbox – and put them back outside when you have finished the test.

You need a plastic test box about 20–40 cm/8–15 in long and 15–30 cm/6–12 in wide. A square or rectangular ice-cream box is ideal, but you can use a small tray or a large margarine or yogurt tub. With a felt pen, draw a line across the bottom to divide it in half, or mark it with a thin piece of tape. Mark the centre of this line with a cross; mark the left half L and the right half R. Put the box on the table in front of you. Make sure it is level and that neither half is in direct sunlight or in any other way more or less attractive to woodlice.

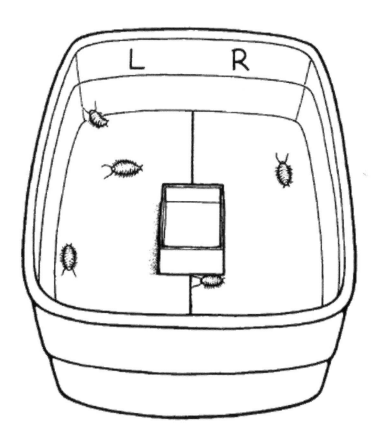

Figure 7.2: A woodlouse testing box.

For the first test, try to influence your woodlice to go Right. Take the first Woodlouse Scoresheet *(page* 148) and fill in 'Right' where it says 'Aim ...'

Your assistant should be ready with the watch and the scoresheet. When you are ready to go, she should open the matchbox, put the open box with all the woodlice in it on the cross in the centre (no, they don't bite!), and start the stopwatch. Her job is to see how well you are doing every 15 seconds.

Woodlouse Scoresheet Aim					
Time (seconds)	15	30	45	60	75
Number in **Left**					
Number in **Right**					
Winner at this time (**L** or **R** or **N**)					

Woodlouse Scoresheet Aim					
Time (seconds)	15	30	45	60	75
Number in **Left**					
Number in **Right**					
Winner at this time (**L** or **R** or **N**)					

After 15 seconds she should say 'Fifteen' and rapidly count how many woodlice have at least one foot in one half of the box. Write down the two numbers and which side wins (e.g. 5 in the **L** row, 3 in the **R** row, and **L** in the bottom row). Then look at the watch and get ready for 30 seconds. With practice you may find you can take a reading every 10 seconds, but counting them and getting the numbers written down is quite tricky.

When there is an equal number in each side, the Assistant should write **N**, since neither side is winning – or leave it blank.

In the mean time, you can try to influence the woodlice in any non-physical way you want. Stare at them; point with all your fingers; shout, 'RIGHT, RIGHT, RIGHT!' No touching the table, the box or them, and no blowing on them.

Carry on for 75 seconds, by which time you will have five results. If they are all hits – that is, all **R** in the first test – then you really seem to be getting somewhere.

But maybe the right side of the box is cooler or darker or otherwise more desirable for woodlice. So, *without moving the box,* do a second test in which you try to get them to go Left. Fill in 'Left' on the second score sheet, then time and score it as before. How did you get on?

If you scored 0 the first time, and five the second, then try to find a better place for your box! If you got 4 or more in the correct direction each time, you are really doing well. Time to swap places and see whether your Assistant has equally good powers of woodlouse control.

Making it More Rigorous

There is a problem with the scientific rigour of this test. Your friend might have wanted you to succeed, and so counted every possible foot in the right half but ignored woodlice that might possibly have just nipped over to the wrong side of the line. Or she might have given you slightly longer than she should to persuade one recalcitrant beast to get across the line. She wouldn't need to be doing this deliberately. Small errors can be made quite unconsciously and still ruin the experiment.

This is easily solved. Before you start, take a dozen or so small pieces of paper. Write **Left** on half of them and **Right** on the rest. Put them into a paper bag or under a cloth. When you are ready to begin, pull one out at random but do not show it to your Assistant or tell her what it says. For your first test try to make the woodlice move this way – silently. Your Assistant cannot be biased in your favour because she does not know which way you are trying to influence them. Obviously you must not shout 'Left' or 'Right', nor point in the direction you want.

For the second 75-second trial, still keeping your paper hidden, try for the opposite direction. When you have finished this too, then you can show her the paper and fill in **Left** or **Right** on the top of the scoresheet. Did you manage to get more woodlice in the right half in this properly controlled test? Did you get five in a row? If so, you are definitely getting somewhere. Now, don't forget to put your woodlice back where you found them.

Tests like this are a lot of fun to do, and you will probably find yourself getting quite worked up over your woodlice. But the tests are hard to assess scientifically. Do the woodlice get bored or sleepy at one end and just stay there? Could you have damaged any of them while putting them in the box? Can you really be sure which side they are all in at a particular moment? You may think up ways to get round these problems and design a better experiment of your own, but problems like these have led many scientists to work with dice or random-number generators.

Tests That Are More Scientific

Dice are the traditional apparatus for testing PK and you can carry out some simple experiments of your own with them.

First you might try for sixes. Throw a die 60 times (or if you have 5 dice throw them, all at once, 12 times; or even 10 dice six times). By chance you should get about 10 sixes.

You might easily get 9 or 11, or perhaps even 8 or 12, but you are very unlikely to get 15 sixes or more.

Percentage chances of throwing various numbers of sixes in 60 throws of the dice

Number of 6s	Fewer than 4	4	5	6	7–13	14	15	16	More than 16
Chance	Less than 1%	2%	4%	8%	Quite likely	8%	4%	2%	Less than 1%

The percentage chances are shown in the table above. As you can see, you are quite likely to roll sixes any-where between 6 and 14 times, but you have minute chances of throwing fewer than 5 sixes, or more than 15. The significant results are those with less than 5 per cent probability.

This shows clearly why parapsychologists have to use statistics. You can conclude that you have PK only if your result is very unlikely to have been just chance.

But – even if you have your statistics right – there is still a problem with this test. Can you see what it is – and how to solve it?

The statistics assume that every face of the die is equally likely to come up on top, but this may not be true. For one thing, you might have been throwing the dice in a special way so as to get more than your fair share of sixes. Some people can do this easily. Indeed, you might like to impress your friends by learning this trick and then trying to convince them that you have psychic powers.

When you set out to do real experiments you must make sure you cannot cheat in this way. A simple solution is to throw the dice from a container (as you find with many board games), or to get someone else to throw them – or both.

A worse problem is that your dice might have been biased.

In fact, most ordinary dice *are* slightly biased. This is because the 'pips' are often hollowed out of the plastic (or wood or whatever) the dice are made of. This means that the 6 face is actually lighter than the others, and the I face is the heaviest. You can imagine that just occasionally, when the die is poised on edge and about to come down to show either 6 or 2, the extra weight of the 2 face might possibly tip the balance.

Although the effect will be very small, it can be significant over many throws. So even if you get a good result – that is, more sixes than you should get by chance – and you were throwing your dice fairly, the high score might be an effect of the bias and nothing to do with PK.

There are at least two ways to try to solve this problem. First you might try to get a perfectly unbiased die. This sounds easy but in fact you are likely to have quite a bit of trouble. You can buy expensive dice that are better than the cheap wooden ones, but you cannot be sure that they are perfectly unbiased unless you do lots of tests. This means throwing the die hundreds of times – and you still might not be totally convinced at the end of it!

Fortunately there is a better way, which is to stop worrying about bias altogether. The problem was that you were always trying for sixes. If you try equally often for each number on the die, then any bias will cancel out. For example, if the bias produces more sixes, you may do well on that part of the test but you will do correspondingly badly when trying for ones. Only a real PK effect can cause the dice to fall in line with all your wishes.

Figure 7.3: It's going to be a six! Have the hollowed-out pips biased the die – or could it be the power of his mind?

We can now design a simple test that should be valid.

A Controlled Dice Experiment

What You Need

- Two people, one to be the Experimenter and one to be the Subject.
- I good-quality die
- A cup or shaker
- A Record Sheet for your results (*see page 154)*

Procedure

Decide who is to be Experimenter and who the Subject. Whoever thinks they have the best PK power should be the Subject first – but you can take turns.

The Experimenter's first job is to decide the order in which you will try for the numbers. This can be decided by throwing the die (it's not likely to be badly biased!) You will see on the Record Sheet a column marked 'Target'. Throw the die and fill in the first number you get in the top space of the Target column. So, for example, if you throw a three first, enter that in the first space. This means that for your first 10 trial throws you will try to get a three.

Then (Experimenter), find the next Target. Throw again and put the number in the next box in the Target column. If you get another three, ignore it and throw again. Carry on like this until you have one of each number in the Target column. These numbers tell you what to aim for.

Now you can begin the test. Hold the shaker and tell the Subject to concentrate on getting a three (or whatever number you have put in the first space). Throw the die and write down the result. Keep encouraging your Subject to think of 'three' while throwing the die another nine times – until you have filled all the spaces in the first row.

Now go on to your second target. If you have written 6 in this space you will now do 10 throws in which your Subject will try to get a six. In this way carry on until you have done all 60 throws and filled in all the Results spaces.

Target	PK Results										Number of hits

Total hits (out of 60)

Results and Analysis

In your Results Sheet, go across each column adding up how many throws were correct. For example, if your target was 5, how many of the throws in that row were fives? Write this total in the right-hand column 'Number of hits'. Add all these hits up to get your final score. If you have got more than 14, or fewer than 6, there is a less than 5 per cent chance that it was just luck. Your Subject might really have been using PK.

Variations on the Dice Experiment

Speeding Up the Experiment

Instead of just using one die at a time you can, if you like, get five dice and throw them all at once, and then once more, for each stage of the experiment. The statistics work just the same way. Does this make any difference to your results?

Some people believe PK is unaffected by the number of dice, and should work just as well with five dice as with one. Others suggest that the effect will be weakened by spreading it out over several dice at once.

Mental Attitude

Did you just stare at the shaker and think about the number you wanted? Or did you shout *'FIVE, FIVE'* at the top of your voice? You might like to invent a test to compare various approaches, to see whether some work better than others.

You can easily get the impression that when you do certain things, the right result follows. For example, if the dice came up 5 just when you shouted the loudest, you might easily begin to think that your shouting caused the hit. In fact, you might have got 5 just by chance. The only way to test your hunches is to do a controlled comparison. By now you can easily see how this should be done. It's always interesting to find out whether or not your own hunches are right – and it's both disappointing and helpful to find out when you are wrong.

Group PK

Can several people trying together exert more PK force than one alone? You can easily do the same dice experiment but this time get a whole group of people to concentrate on the die and try to make it come out the way they all want. You might like to try this in class at school or college, or with a group of friends at home. In this case the Experimenter must shout out the number you are all going to aim for – and make sure everyone is trying to get the same result.

Competitive PK

Can one person's wishes cancel out another's? Get one person to try for a number while another person tries for the opposite number (look on any die and you will see that 6 is opposite 1, 2 is opposite 5, and 3 is opposite 4). What difference does this make? You might like to set up competitions between boys and girls, or believers and non-believers, and see who does best.

So next time you are walking along the street and the traffic lights change as you come to them, what will you think? Do you still think you can use your mind to influence things out there, or is it all self-delusion?

How about those PK Superstars?

The man who put PK on television was Uri Geller. He has been hailed as a psychic superstar, and denounced as a fraud. We may never know the whole truth. He maintains that

▶

all his powers are psychic and that he bends spoons using only his mind. James Randi and others say that they can bring about the same results by normal conjuring tricks, and therefore that Geller's powers are not paranormal. You will have to make up your own mind.

Geller's appearance on the scene sparked off dozens of claims by children, often called 'mini-Gellers', that they too could bend spoons. At the University of Bath Professor Harry Collins investigated some of these children, asking them to try to bend spoons in a psychology laboratory. During each test he asked the observer deliberately to relax vigilance for a time – only during those times were spoons bent.

They thought no one was looking, but unfortunately a camera was. What he had not told the children was that he had a camera set up behind a one-way mirror. He managed to photograph several of the children in the act of bending spoons under their feet, or using both hands...

The film of Madame Kulagina in action shows her leaning right over the table on which the objects were moving, so that her face and capacious bosom were within inches of them. Clearly she was not touching them with her hands, and she did not appear to be blowing them with her mouth, either. However, the objects she moved – a metal bar and a compass needle – would definitely be influenced by a magnet. She could easily have had a magnet in her mouth, or tucked into her clothing. We have no evidence to show, one way or the other, the source of her powers.

Occam's Razor

William of Occam (or Ockham) was a fourteenth-century philosopher who laid one of the foundations of modern scientific

▶

thought. His 'razor', or principle, sometimes called the Law of Parsimony, was that the scientist seeking to explain something should always look for the simplest sensible explanation – or to be precise, that *for purposes of explanation things not known to exist should not, unless it is absolutely necessary, be postulated as existing.* Thus we say that a helium-filled balloon floats upward because helium is less dense than air, rather than because a band of small and invisible angels is lifting it.

We have no evidence that there is no band of angels, but we have no evidence *for* them either, and to invent them merely to explain this phenomenon seems unnecessary. We know from other tests that helium is less dense than air; so the density explanation is enough to explain the behaviour of the balloon – and we should always choose the simplest sensible explanation we have.

William of Occam would probably choose, had he seen the film, to explain the movement of Kulagina's objects in terms of a hidden magnet rather than in terms of PK – for we have no evidence that PK exists, whereas we do know that magnets exist and would perform this trick. In other words, there is no need to postulate the existence of PK to explain the observations.

Rolf Alexander's 'cloud-busting' was examined in detail and discussed at length by meteorologist Dr Richard Scorer from the Imperial College of Science and Technology. Scorer watched Alexander in action and said afterwards

Apparently he only 'works' with fair-weather cumulus clouds, and clouds of this type disappear in about 20 minutes anyway...When such clouds disappear their

▶

place is usually taken by others of very similar appearance, and unless this fact is known it is quite easy for an untrained observer to believe that what is seen is still the same cloud... The simplest explanation [for Alexander's claims] is that when alone he has discovered that clouds of this type at which he looks intently disappear. When examining the rest of the sky, when he has finished, he finds that it looks very much the same as before and concludes that he has been responsible for the dissolution of the cloud. The experiment can be repeated over and over again on a suitable day.

The weird goings-on in Cox's garage in Rolla, Missouri, were dismissed by psychical investigator Tony Cornell. Cornell suggested that the films of apparently paranormal activity were taken by single-frame photography with the fish-tank removed. In other words, he said, the sealing of the fish tank was an illusion; it could easily be removed and the contents manipulated. So Cox and/or Richards, according to Cornell, first exposed one frame of film of a deflated balloon in the tank. Then the fish tank was taken off, the balloon blown up a little, the fish tank replaced, and a second frame of film taken. Then the fish tank was removed, the balloon inflated a little more, the fish tank replaced, and a third frame taken. Thus, over a long period of time they could have produced a film of a balloon apparently blowing itself up inside the fish tank.

As evidence to support his hypothesis, Cornell produced enlarged sections of the Rolla film in which the fish tank was absent from one or two frames. In other words, either it had mysteriously disappeared for about 1/24 of a second or (after manipulating the contents) the camera operator had forgotten to put it back for one of the frames! Cornell also produced

▶

his own witty film 'Twentieth Century Cox', in which he used single-frame photography to reproduce many of the phenomena seen on the Rolla films.

As for Ted Serius and his 'thoughtography', a plausible explanation was put forward by two photographic experts from New York, David Eisendrath and Charles Reynolds. Ted usually held a little black tube in front of the lens when he was 'working' – he called it his 'gizmo' – and they said he might have occasionally concealed in the tube a little novelty lens and picture, of the type that can be bought in gift shops to hang on key rings. Hold the lens up to your eye and you can see the Eiffel Tower, or various other famous views. Hold one of these in front of the lens of an instant camera with a small flashlight, such as used in Ted's performances, and you get on film something just like one of his thoughtographs. We have made them ourselves, and quite surprising they are too.

Remember Occam's Razor: the fact that something is surprising does not necessarily mean that it must be paranormal! Indeed, we should not postulate the existence of PK unless there is no simpler explanation.

8

The Ouija Board

The ouija board is one of the best-known ways of 'communicating with the spirits'. There are several different kinds of ouija board, but they all have in common some kind of pointer that can indicate a sequence of words, numbers, or letters, and so spell out messages.

The name 'ouija' is simply a mixture of the French and German words for yes *(oui* and *ja)*. Its simplest use is to answer YES/NO questions, although it is more often used to spell out whole words. Although the origins of the board are lost in the mists of time, it has certainly been used for hundreds of years, and thousands of people have been deeply affected by it.

History of Ouija

The ouija board seems to have been used in China since Confucius (about 500 BC), and also, at around the same time, by the Greek mathematician Pythagoras and his strange school of 300 young acolytes at Croton in southern Italy.

A group of Roman soldiers supposedly used the ouija board to predict the name of the next emperor – it said Theodosius. Unfortunately they failed to keep the secret, and were tried for treason. Theodosius was less lucky; he was executed.

During the Second World War the composer Rudolph Friml claimed that by using his ouija board he communicated regularly with Chopin and other dead composers, not to mention Napoleon, who assured him that Germany would lose the war.

One of the most intriguing stories of the ouija board occurred during the First World War. A group of captured British soldiers made an ouija board in a Turkish prison camp. They managed to persuade their guards that 'the Spook' was real and powerful, and as a result were able to escape from the camp. The full story is told in the book *The Road to En-Dor*, written by E. H. Jones in 1920.

In 1966 Parker Brothers brought out an ouija board as a game in the US, and in the following year sold two million of them – more even than *Monopoly* sets!

A 17-year-old American woman was told by her ouija board that her boyfriend had been shot at in Vietnam. She gathered that he was riding in a jeep with another GI; a shot rang out and the torch he was holding was knocked out of his hand. Worried, she wrote to him about this and – the story goes – the incident happened, just as described, while her letter was on its way to him.

A 1983 survey suggested that 30 per cent of practitioners use ouija boards to communicate with dead people; almost as many to get in touch with living people; and the rest are trying to reach pets, spirits, angels, or other non-human intelligences. Among the most common spirits to announce themselves are those of Jesus, St John, Socrates, and Abraham Lincoln.

A student at Oxford University regularly used the ouija board with a group of friends. One night she had held her finger on the glass for several hours, almost continuously. Towards the end of the session a troublesome 'spirit' appeared, and none of the group liked what it was saying. They challenged the 'spirit', who suddenly refused to move the glass any more – and disappeared.

Everyone snatched their hands away, but this girl's arm remained stuck out in front of her. She could not put it down. It was paralysed and numb and she was terrified it would stay that way; indeed, she was convinced that the spirit had come out of the glass and got hold of her. Eventually, however, the feeling came back and she was able to move it again.

In 1994 Stephen Young was found guilty of the horrible murder of a newlywed couple in Wadhurst, England. However, it was later discovered that four members of the jury had used an ouija board to try to contact one of the victims and help them decide whether or not Stephen was guilty. As a result the verdict was quashed by three Appeal Court Judges. Although he was subsequently retried, found guilty and sentenced, public debate about the ouija board incident ensued. Some people argued that it was all a fuss about nothing – the jury were only having a bit of fun while locked up in a hotel for the night awaiting the rest of the trial. But others believed that the ouija board might really have influenced the jury's decision, and no decision on something so important should be affected by something as frivolous as an ouija board.

This case illustrates the possible dangers of using the ouija board. It certainly can be dangerous – and this need not be because there are any spirits pushing the pointer around. The danger lies in taking too seriously the suggestions that come from it.

We could argue that no one should ever use the ouija board again because of its dangers. In fact we know that school children, college students and adults have been using various forms of ouija for decades, and will almost certainly go on doing so. Rather than pontificating that no one should touch it, therefore, we prefer to suggest ways in which the ouija board can be used sensibly and safely, and how to avoid the worst dangers it can throw at you.

The Planchette

In 1853 a French spiritualist, M Planchette, invented an instrument similar to the ouija board; it became known as a *planchette* – which means 'little plank'. It was a heart-shaped board about 15 cm/6 in across, with three legs; two had casters on and the third was an ordinary lead pencil. The pencil was slipped through a rubber-lined hole in the point of the heart.

At that time, spiritualism was a new craze. Mediums were springing up all over the place and arranging dark seances in which the 'sitters' collected around an ordinary table, placed their hands on it and then waited for the spirits to start work. If they were lucky the table tipped and even danced about in reply to their questions. If they were even more lucky they heard voices, felt cold breezes and saw luminous objects floating about in the dark.

But many people wanted more direct communication with the spirits. They wanted to be able to ask questions and get more than 'one thump for yes, two for no'. They sometimes called out the letters of the alphabet one by one and waited for the table to tap at a letter, before beginning again. This must have been extremely tedious. They even tried fixing a pencil to the table leg in an attempt to get it to write. This, then, was the origin of the 'little plank'. By 1868 planchettes were appearing in great numbers in booksellers' shops in the US. Some even had patent insulated casters and other special devices to 'tempt' the spirits.

The planchette is used in a way similar to the ouija board. The sitters rest their fingers on the planchette and it will usually circle around the table and then begin to write, apparently all on its own. The advantage is that you are not restricted to the letters and numbers you provide. Also, the planchette may be able to write letters much more quickly than the ouija board's pointer can find them. One big problem is that its writing may be hard to read. Another is that it gets through an awful lot of paper!

In the 1860s the planchette was called 'the despair of science'. Now it is largely forgotten, but the ouija board remains.

Making an Ouija Board

There are many variations, but the most common version uses a glass for the pointer, sliding on a table. Several people sit around the table with their fingers resting lightly on the top of the upturned glass. The glass is then able to move freely around and point to words or letters placed around the edges of the table.

The ideal table is quite small, perhaps 60 cm (2 ft) square, or a rectangle 60 x 90 cm (2 ft x 3 ft). The surface is far more important than the size; it must be as smooth as possible. Finely polished wood makes a good surface, as does laminate or formica, as long as it is really clean. Bare wood, or wood treated with any sticky varnish or paint will not work well, nor will tables covered with soft plastic material or any kind of textured surface. Glass can be used – and would be perfect for some experiments – but the sound the glass pointer makes sliding on it sets my teeth on edge so badly that I'd never use it!

If you don't have a suitable table or if you want to make a special ouija board, get a piece of wood – or preferably MDF (Medium Density Fibreboard) – of the right size. Alternatively a piece of laminate will do, or even cardboard as long as it is thick and strong enough. The advantage of using a separate surface like this is that you can draw the letters directly on to it, which will make some of the experiments easier to carry out. However, you do not need to make a special board.

Having chosen your table you need a pointer. The usual pointer is an ordinary kitchen glass. Choose your glass carefully. A wine glass tends to tip over if it meets the tiniest sticky patch. Beer mugs are too heavy and will not move easily. Best is probably a small plain drinking glass with sides that slope slightly outwards, so that it is stable yet light. A small cup may also work well. Try out a few combinations, pushing the glass or cup around until you find one that moves over the surface smoothly and easily.

Next you need to make the letters. If you are making your own special board out of wood or card you can write the letters directly on to the surface. This is quick and easy, and you can make the letters as simple or elegant as you like.

The traditional way to make the letters is to take lots of little pieces of paper and write the letters on them. If you are going to do this we suggest you do it properly, especially if you want to do some real experiments. Use thick, stiff paper or thin card, and cut a set of pieces all exactly the same size. Decide how many you need before you begin. You will certainly need all the letters of the alphabet. You may also like to have the digits from

0 to 9

which are good for asking about dates and even for addresses and telephone numbers. The words

YES and NO

are useful and save a lot of time, and some people also like to have

DON'T KNOW

which can double for a question mark. You might even like to add a punctuation mark or two. If you used all the letters, numbers, essential words and a full stop, you would need 40 pieces of paper. So decide what you need before you start cutting.

Once all your letters are made, lay them carefully around the table. You can arrange them however you like, but try to keep any that are likely to be confused

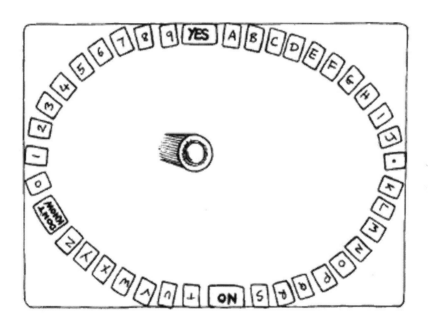

Figure 8.1 : One way to lay out the letters for a homemade ouija board.

well apart from each other. This applies most of all to

YES and NO

they are best put on opposite sides of the table.

Finally, you need some means of recording any messages that appear. You can use a tape recorder and leave it running. This has the advantage that it records what everyone says – which often includes how they interpret messages. The disadvantage is that you have to listen to the whole tape all over again – and that can mean many hours of tedious listening.

Simply writing down the messages is probably better. Writing while keeping your hand on the glass can be difficult; so the best method is to have a separate person to act as 'scribe'. If you are scribe, make sure you write each letter down at once, for human memory is tricky and after even a few minutes different people will remember different versions of the same event.

Also, write down every single letter or number the glass points to. It is no good just writing down the ones that seem to make sense at the time. Often what looks like nonsense to begin with starts to make sense after a while. Also, some of the most interesting 'messages' are the ones you find only when you look more carefully at the record, after the session is over. Finally, if you want to do serious experiments, you must get into the habit of recording *accurately.*

Making a Planchette

What you need is a small piece of rigid material such as plywood or plastic, supported horizontally so that it glides easily over the table, with a pencil, ballpoint pen or felt-tip pen stuck to it and resting on the paper. The traditional Victorian planchettes comprised an elegant heart-shaped piece of polished wood running on delicate casters, but with modern materials there are much simpler possibilities.

One simple method is to use an old plastic tub with a snap-on lid – the kind that is made for margarine, houmous or cottage cheese. Using scissors or a knife, make a hole just big enough for a ballpoint pen in the centre of the lid, and another in the centre of the base.

Put the lid on the tub and poke a ballpoint pen up through both holes, until the point sticks out of the top by about 1 cm (½ in). Note (or mark) where on the pen is just level with the bottom of the tub. Open the tub and wrap a rubber band four or five times around the ballpoint pen at this place. Now put the pen back in, with the rubber band inside, and put the lid back on the tub. When the tub rests upside-down on a piece of paper the pen sticks out through the lid, but when you put your fingers on the base the lid will rest flat on the paper and the pen will press down hard. You can now operate the tub like the pointer on an ouija board.

Using your Ouija Board

You could say that ouija boards are a bit like fireworks. They can be a lot of fun but you should understand their dangers and treat them with respect.

Some people say ouija boards are dangerous because they call up the spirits – and the lowest kinds of spirits at that. Others say they are dangerous because they call on the collective unconscious of all the people at the table. Either way you could be playing with 'fire'. In the unconscious parts of all our minds lurk those motivations we would not like to own up to, those desires we would rather not possess, and those fears that we hesitate to express. If these are going to come up in the messages from the ouija board you need to tackle them with quite as much skill and care as you would any spirit.

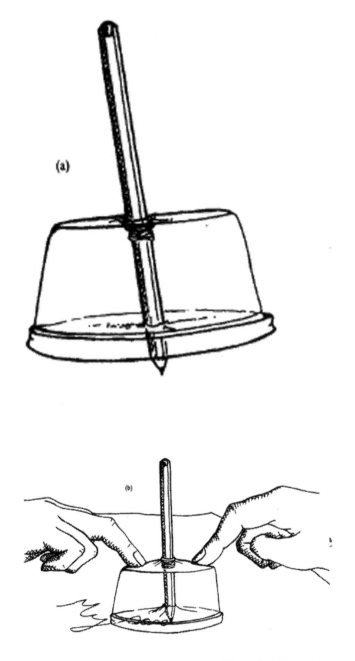

Figure 8.2: A modem planchette. The ballpoint pen goes through both base and lid of the plastic tub. (a) A rubber band holds the pen down so that (b) when you put your fingers on the tub, the pen presses firmly on the paper.

Our suggestions are, if you don't really want to use the ouija board, don't! If you really do want to use the ouija board, always treat it as though there was someone in the glass. Even if you think the messages are really coming from the people sitting around you, treat the glass with respect. Speak to it as though it were a real person. Do not say rude things or shout at it. Do not snatch your hand away in the middle of a message. This way, you should have no trouble. Bear this in mind before you begin. It will not spoil your fun.

The ouija board works best with several people. So invite three or four friends to come and help you with your new instrument. Don't pick someone whom you think will be frightened by it, and *never* use it to scare anyone. The best group is probably four or five people who all get on well together and have no particular enmities or quarrels to get in the way. You can take it in turns to be scribe.

Figure 8.3: Each person has a finger on the upturned glass in this homemade ouija board. Be careful: ouija boards can be frightening or dangerous if not treated with respect.

Sit round the table and make sure that everyone can reach the top of the glass, even when it moves to the letter furthest away from him or her. The room should be dimly lit, but light enough for you all to see the letters and for the scribe to keep the record. You may find that soft lighting and atmospheric music help. Or you may prefer to have silence – or your favourite album. Try it and see.

Each person should put one or two fingers on the pointer. Now deliberately push the glass around a little, so that you all know how it feels when it moves. Then stop pushing and begin the session.

Traditional questions to begin with are 'Is there anyone there?' or 'Are there any messages for us?' You might ask 'Is there anyone in the glass?'

The glass may start to move immediately or it may take a while. If it seems to be stuck and doesn't move at all for several minutes, you can always give it a little push just to start it off. As long as you get a

YES

to this first question, you can carry on.

If you believe the pointer is controlled by a spirit or spirits, you might like to ask who is there, or who is in control. Even if you don't believe in spirits it is best to act as though there is someone in there. You could check on whether there is any intelligence at work by asking it to spell out your middle name – or the name of your town, or the number of the house.

Don't *forget to write down every letter that comes!*

After a while you should feel that the pointer has a life of its own and moves quickly about the board, apparently without being pushed by anyone. This feels rather odd, exciting, perhaps creepy. Don't be frightened by the movement – allow the pointer to flow. Even if there are spirits, they cannot harm you directly.

Some people hope that the board may somehow show insight, and therefore be useful in taking decisions – perhaps about romance or plans for the future. Others may have simpler goals, and may want to try asking which horse is going to win the 3.30 tomorrow. (And if your ouija board can give you the right answer to that one, please write and let us know!) But remember, there are some questions it is better not to ask.

For example, suppose that Jonathan is about to take an important exam for which he has prepared well. But suppose he is seriously worried about failing, consults the ouija board, and is told he is going to fail – and he believes this. He might become deeply depressed. He might well fail the exam because he is now convinced he will do so. He might even contemplate suicide. If all this were to happen, then the ouija board would have ruined his life.

Just don't ask stupid questions. And if someone else does, then don't take the answers too seriously.

Ending your session correctly is also important. When you have had enough of a particular 'spirit', don't forget to say goodbye and thank you. This way you will close off anything that has been going on. In your own subconscious mind the session is ended, and your own mind is less likely to play tricks on you.

If by any chance you get 'spirits' you don't like, act the same way. Don't just get frightened and pull your hands away; otherwise, in your own subconscious, you may still believe there is something there, even if there isn't. Instead, be firm with your 'spirit'. You might say 'We don't want to speak to you any more. Please go away. We are going to take our hands off now.' If you observe these simple principles using the ouija board will be much more fun.

How the Ouija Board Might Work

The spiritualist explanation is that there are spirits all around us. The ouija board is merely a channel that allows them to communicate with us. They are clairvoyant and telepathic, and omniscient, and so they are able not only to spell out middle names but also to read our thoughts and predict the winners of tomorrow's races.

Many people have tried to make scientific sense out of spiritualism. In 1863 Samuel Guppy wrote that the human body is a condensation of gases which constantly exude from the skin an invisible vapour, otherwise known as electricity, and that the fingers coming in contact with the pointer transmit to it an 'odic force' which sets it in motion. This does not appear to throw much light on the question of how it works.

The spiritualist theory is that the spirits somehow use our bodies. This is the basis of the term 'medium'. The spirits cannot speak without human mouths, or move things without human limbs, so they need a 'medium' through which to transmit the force. The medium does nothing more than allow the spirits to come through. In the case of the ouija board, all the people round the table are acting as mediums. They are, if you believe the spiritualist theory, forming a conduit through which the spirits move the glass.

An alternative theory is that no spirits are involved at all. The glass moves because all the people round it are unconsciously pushing it. The messages make sense because they come from the unconscious minds of all the people whose fingers are resting on the glass.

This second theory has a lot of evidence in its favour. We know that all human beings have great difficulty in restraining tiny twitches of their hands – and we are largely unaware of those twitches. Our bodies move all the time, even when we are trying to stand still, and it needs clever feedback mechanisms to keep us in a steady position. We may not realize it, but our bodies are constantly drifting away from where we want them to be. As soon as we detect a movement, for example by seeing or feeling it, our muscles automatically cut in to put things right. Otherwise we would fall over.

A little experiment: try standing perfectly still. Can you feel the little twitches of your muscles as those automatic mechanisms operate? Now try it with your eyes shut, and feel for those twitches in your feet and legs. Keeping upright is much harder when you can't see every movement. These same feedback mechanisms may be crucial on the ouija board.

People who have used the ouija board generally say that they had nothing to do with the movements – they just kept their hands still, or allowed them to follow the pointer. But no one can keep his or her hands completely still, or follow a movement completely smoothly. So all that is required is for the glass to start moving – perhaps one person 'helps a little', or another gets tired and her hand slips a bit – and the pointer will gather momentum. No one wants to hold the glass back – so they all slightly anticipate its next move. Although no one realizes it, each person may be contributing a little to the movement – by 'unconscious muscular action'.

The first person to test this theory was the brilliant nineteenth-century scientist Michael Faraday, who for many years was a star performer at the Royal Institution in London. He was famous for his studies of electricity and magnetism, and appalled by the credulous public's belief in spiritualism. He had seen tables tipping and turning, and wanted to demonstrate definitively whether the spirits were moving the tables or whether the sitters' own hands were doing the work.

He stuck little pieces of cardboard on a table, under the sitters' hands, with a special kind of glue. This glue allowed the card to move slightly in one direction, but not to move back again. So, after the table had moved, he could see which had moved first – the table or the hand.

The spiritualists, naturally, claimed that the table moved first. They were quite convinced that they kept their hands still and did nothing. His experiments proved that their hands actually moved first. The sitters hadn't realized it, but they were pushing the table.

He added a clever twist to his experiments. He made a little indicator out of a straw which showed immediately whenever one of the sitters' hands moved. As soon as they could see this indicator, all the movements stopped. It seems that the spiritualists honestly believed they were not moving their hands and did not intend to cheat. However, the way you keep still is by counteracting the little movements you inevitably make. As soon as the indicator showed them their own little movements, they stopped.

Faraday also realized that holding out your arm for a long time makes it even harder to feel any little movements, and the semi-darkness makes it hard to see them. This is just the same with the ouija board. When you have tried it you will realize how tired your arm gets. You can no longer be sure whether you are moving the glass or not, and it is all too easy to become convinced that a spirit is doing it.

Where, then, do all the messages come from? If there are no spirits they must be coming from the minds of the people present. This could either be just one person's mind, or it could be some kind of co-ordinated effect of several minds working together. Psychologists understand little about how one mind could affect the precise movements of a glass, let alone how several minds might move it together. Here lie unknown waters – and the potential for being surprised, amused and also frightened by an ouija board or planchette. I wouldn't play frivolously with the unknown depths of my own mind, let alone several other people's.

Ouija Board Experiments

Can the glass tell you something you couldn't possibly have known? If it can, then you could not have been unconsciously pushing it to the right letters.

The simplest test is to ask the glass some questions to which no one in the group knows the answer. You can be as inventive as you like with this one. You might ask for the birthday of someone not present, or where they lived as a child. Such questions are easy to check later, but the problem is that one of you might, subconsciously, have known the answer.

We all know far more than we can consciously remember, and the ouija board is an ideal situation for such forgotten memories to come out. This phenomenon is called 'cryptomnesia' or 'hidden memory'. A good experiment must rule this out.

A favourite ouija test is to ask the spirits where they died and of what, and when and where they were buried. I have spent many fruitless hours searching through the graveyards where 'spirits' told me their bodies lay. I have never found one that was true. However, even if you did find one the possibility exists that one of the group had seen the gravestone or read about the person in a local history book. Cryptomnesia can include everything you have ever read or heard or seen. To rule it out is difficult – but not impossible.

A better test is to set up some event that none of you can see. For example, get a friend to go into another room and do something silly. Presumably the spirits, if they exist, ought to be able to see this and report it to you.

Can you see the problem with this? If the friend goes off and tries to think up something silly to do, they may easily come up with the same silly idea as you do. Then the glass will get the right answer because you all think along similar lines.

The way round this one is to do a proper randomization, as we have done with previous experiments. Give your friend a die and ask her to go away and think up half a dozen silly things to do and write them down. She might write 1 : Stand on a chair. 2: Mouth the words of 'Jingle Bells'. 3: Pretend to be swimming – and so on. At a prearranged time she should throw the die and do whatever her list instructs her to do. Once you have an answer from the glass you can go and ask her whether it was right.

To be sure of your result you should do this test twice. If your glass gives you the right answer twice running, you can be fairly sure that it was not just luck.

In the light of previous experiments you may be able to think of refinements to this test. However, there will always be one outstanding problem: even if you get good results these could be explained in lots of different ways. For example, it could be telepathy or clairvoyance between the living, rather than the effects of spirits. In fact you will have learned little about spirits or the ouija board itself this way.

A more interesting experiment is closely related to Faraday's original idea. Oddly enough almost no experiments on ouija have been done since his time. So you could be breaking new ground if you carry out ouija experiments properly.

A Scientific Test

You can try to discover for yourself whether or not the pointer is really controlled by the spirits or by your own hands. If Faraday was right, the sitters must be able to see the letters in order to spell out messages. So if they were blindfolded the ouija board would not work. On the other hand, if the spirits are in control, blindfolding should make no difference. Presumably they alone need to see the letters, and they can see through walls, under pieces of card and indeed all over the place.

The problem with blindfolding is that the glass may just rush about the place, knocking the letters aside, falling off the table and generally making the experiment difficult. A better method is to use concealed letters. The basic principle is to set up a code that any spirit can easily read, although the sitters cannot.

Method 1
Take all your letters off the table and turn them upside down. It now becomes important that you made them properly and that they are all the same size and shape, so that you cannot tell one from the others. Spread them all out and shuffle them thoroughly. When you no longer know where any of the letters are, write a number on the back of each card, from 1 to 40 (or however many there are).

Now place them around the table again, as before but still face-down in order from 1 to 40. All you will be able to see is the numbers, and you should have no idea which letter or word is where. Make quite sure nobody peeps at any letters. You now have a ouija board which consists of letters and numbers that you cannot see, but presumably the spirits can. If they are really as all-seeing as people claim, this little deception should present them with no problem at all. They can still use your arms and hands, but you cannot be putting your own ideas and unconscious wishes on the board. Indeed, it might even be better for the spirits to use it this way.

So try it.

As before, get the glass going. Speak to the glass as though there really were someone in there and ask a series of simple questions. The answers won't immediately make sense. For example, you might ask 'What's your name?' and get the answer '7, 34, 2, 8, 17'. Persevere until you have at least a few answers and write them down exactly as they happen. The scribe's job is very important here.

Perhaps an even better method is to enlist the help of a favourite 'spirit' before you begin. Suppose you have been communicating with 'Antigone'. You could, with the letters all visible, ask 'Antigone' whether she would like to take part in an experiment and whether she thinks she will be able to see the letters even when you cannot. If she says 'Yes', then you can proceed with the experiment.

When you have enough answers, thank the 'spirit' and let it go. Now you can turn over all the letters and decode your message. Does it make sense? Does '7, 34, 2, 8, 17' decode into 'KYLIE' or 'KFUNR'? If the answers really came from a spirit then it should make a real name, or close enough. What do you conclude? Did you need to be able to see the letters, or could the spirits do it for you?

Method 2
A problem with the previous method is that you can do it only once. You could write the numbers in pencil and rub them out, but this is fiddly and some marks might remain. If you want to do the experiment more than once the following method is better.

Make a ouija board with a circular ring of letters and numbers on a single piece of paper – 40 characters in all. Make another sheet of thick paper or cardboard to fit over the first, so that you cannot see through and the one below is completely hidden. On the top sheet write the numbers 1, 2, 3 and so on up to 40 around the rim, over the characters below.

If you made a specialized ouija board and wrote the letters on it, then you need only make the top ring and place it on top of your circle of letters – but you'll need some tape or something to hold it in place.

Then you need to turn the lower ring round by an unknown amount. Ideally get someone not in the group to do it while the sitters are all out of the room. Now each of the numbers you can see is above a character – but none of you knows which one.

Have a session, ask questions, and simply write down the numbers you get. When you have enough answers stop, see which letter lies below Number 1, and then write out a complete correspondence list. Then, as before, see whether your 'messages' make sense.

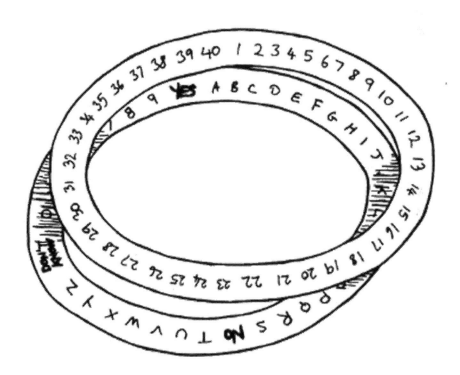

Figure 8.4: Setting up a simple code. You cannot see the letters but the spirits should have no trouble communicating under these conditions.

If you do one of these experiments you ought to be able to make up your own mind about the ouija board. Were you unconsciously pushing it, or were there really spirits in the glass?

Is It True?

There is no doubt that ouija sessions can be fun, and scary, and that the messages which appear to come from the board may be silly or disturbingly accurate. But there are few properly substantiated cases that show any evidence, apart from the fact that some people are more suggestible than others. The remarkable story of the American woman and her boyfriend in Vietnam reached us without any names or addresses; there is no way we can check the facts.

The story about the student is certainly true; it happened to one of us! But the reason was almost certainly psychological and nothing to do with spirits. After two or three hours of holding your arm outstretched in one position you cannot feel exactly where it is. All the nerves that normally give messages to the brain have long ago stopped responding properly, and so the arm feels numb and disconnected. In addition, if you have spent several hours trying not to move your arm, and convincing yourself that a spirit is doing it, it is hard instantly to stop being convinced. The numb arm really does feel as though a spirit has taken it over. There is little danger in any of this, and it all wears off quite soon. The only danger lies in *believing* it is dangerous.

Michael Faraday's experiments 150 years ago showed that objects were moved by human muscles. More recent experiments may explain how the ouija board can give those uncannily meaningful messages.

▶

The Curious Case of Philip, the Imaginary Ghost

In the early 1970s, a group from the Toronto Society for Psychical Research set out to 'create' a ghost. They met regularly and invented a complete history for Philip, a rather silly English aristocrat of the seventeenth century.

In subsequent seances they found they could easily communicate with the 'spirit of Philip', who seemed, by rapping and movements of the table, to provide all sorts of fascinating insights to the history they had created for him.

Clearly Philip was not an existing spirit, since they had deliberately invented him – and yet they were apparently able to communicate with him. So their own minds must, consciously or unconsciously, have been providing the answers. They were well aware of what they were doing, and yet they went on communicating with this imaginary spirit for more than five years.

The human mind has more depth than most people realize. In fact, to paraphrase J. B. S. Haldane, the human mind is not only stranger than we imagine; it is stranger than we *can* imagine!

It is also capable of irrational belief. Beware: remember that the ouija board's messages may be the result of human imagination; do not believe that it tells the truth. The worst danger of the ouija board is to take its messages too seriously.

9

Palmistry

People seem to have been telling the future by reading hands for 5,000 years – there are mentions of the practice in ancient Chinese and Indian writings – and stories abound on the efficacy of the ancient art. Aristotle is said to have practised palm-reading, and may around 340 BC have read and foretold the amazing future of his pupil Alexander the Great.

One of the most famous practitioners and popularizers of hand-reading was the nineteenth-century Count Louis Hamon, who called himself Cheiro. He read the hands of the rich and famous in the 1890s, and apparently foretold countless events including the exact dates of the deaths of Queen Victoria, Edward VII and Lord Kitchener.

Hand-reading is relatively simple – it requires no apparatus – and yet it throws up some of the most bizarre experiences of all. Consider the case of John Snell. As a young man John went into the army and went on active service to India, where he visited a fair or *mela*. While he was there he had his hand read by a fakir under the shade of a mango tree.

The fakir said he could see the young man meeting a beautiful woman and falling in love; he could see him being successful in his life; and then suddenly he went quiet and said he could see no more. John told him to go on – what could he see in later life? The fakir was most reluctant to say anything, but John complained loudly that he had paid his rupee and expected a proper reading. The fakir hesitantly said he could see John's death – that he would die on his 40th birthday.

John dismissed the incident – after all, fakirs can say anything, and this was only someone in a fairground. He carried on with his life, left the army, and did indeed meet and marry a lovely woman. He became a truck-driver, and life was good. But as the years rolled by he remembered the old man's prophecy. In his 39th year he stopped drinking Guinness.

As his 40th birthday approached he began to worry, and went to his doctor for a check-up. He was perfectly well, but he could not help feeling apprehensive. On the eve of his birthday he could not sleep. In the morning he lingered in bed, called in sick and did not go to work, instead staying at home all day.

Nothing happened.

He felt a little foolish, although still rather worried.

The following night his father went down to the pub and was greeted by the landlord with condolences: 'I was sorry to hear the news, Mr Snell.'

'What news?'

'About your son. I heard he died...'

When they finally sorted things out, they discovered that, quite unknown to the family, there had been another John Snell living in the next street – and the other John Snell had died on *his* 40th birthday.

So did the fakir read the right death in the wrong hand?

Palmistry at Parties

Whether or not you believe that our hands hold the secrets of life, and can therefore be used to predict the future, palmistry is great fun to try with your friends and at parties.

Often I find that when I get to a party there are lots of interesting people but I don't know many of them, and find it difficult to begin talking to people. 'Do you come here often?' gets boring after a time. Other people can be shy too, even if they'd really like someone to talk to. But offer to read someone's hand, and you are on to a winner. First of all, it gives you both something to do and you don't have to stare into one another's faces, which can be quite difficult. Second, you don't have to understand much about palmistry – or even say much – to interest the other person. This means you can do it even when conversation is difficult – in spite of loud music, or when the other person doesn't speak the same language as you.

Most people quite like having their hands read, and don't take it too seriously. Three times out of four you can within minutes be holding the hand of the person you fancy, and be finding out some useful facts. For example, you can say, 'I see some childhood illnesses here...how old are you now?' Or you can say, 'I see June is an important time of the year for you. When is your birthday?' or 'You seem to be rather artistic – what sort of things do you like?' No matter if they laugh and say they aren't artistic at all! You have still broken the ice and begun to talk.

One tip: don't take it too seriously yourself– or force it on people. It's a good way to get to know people, but don't become a palmistry bore.

What's in the Hands?

The hands are supposed to reveal details of seven different aspects of life.

According to the experts, the left hand holds the destiny we were born with; the right shows what we do with our talents and with that future. At least, this is so for right-handed people; if you are left-handed, the opposite is the case.

The shapes of our hands, and the lines on our skin, are largely given to us with our genes – we inherit them from our parents. So, like many other characteristics, they are pre-set– but within limits. One example is your height. To a large extent you inherit your height, at least if you have plenty of food when you are growing up. If you are malnourished you will not grow to your full potential – and then your height will depend on the environment more than on your genes.

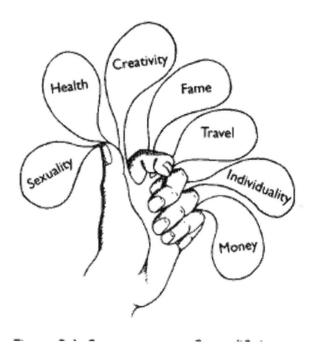

Figure 9.1: Seven aspects of your life in your hand.

Or take the lines on your face. You grow up looking a bit like your parents, but as time goes by the experiences of your own unique life begin to tell on your face. Have you ever noticed how the lines and wrinkles of very old people seem to reflect their character? It is as though someone who has been smiling all his life ends up with smily wrinkles, while the miserable complaining types end up with those down-curved lines round the side of their mouths which make them look permanently cross.

All this could be said of the hands, too – but palmistry claims more than that. It claims that the left hand holds our destiny, that there are recorded the things that will inevitably happen to us, however hard we try to avoid them. *'Somewhere in the Great Book,'* they say, *'It is written that on 14 March next year you will...'* This is hard to disprove, and certainly if your left hand accurately predicts your life then perhaps there is some truth in it. But if the future is already written there, then there is no free will...

However, there are always differences between left and right hands, and according to palmists these show that we can exert some influence over our future. The other hand, the right, signifies potential and the changes we can make in our lives; some say the hand itself develops through life as we gain experience. The effect is to reveal how well or badly we are responding to life's challenges – whether we are building on our strengths or giving in to our worst weaknesses.

Some say that the right hand is to do with work and the open side of life, while the left hand belongs to the spiritual – the dark side. To others the right means the conscious and the left the unconscious or hidden side of our natures. In Latin, the right hand is *dexter*, from which come the words dextrous and dexterity, while the left hand is *sinister*.

Palmists traditionally read the left hand first – perhaps because it shows what we were born with, or perhaps because it is nearest the heart.

There are two distinct things to look at – the size, shape and structure of the hand, and the lines on the palm. The

Greek word for hand is χειρ, or *cheir,* and the word *cheirognomy* is sometimes used to describe study of the shape of the hand, the size and flexibility of the fingers and so on, and sometimes for the study of the character as revealed by the hand. Meanwhile *cheirosophy* sometimes refers to the mystical marks on the skin of the palm. The whole art of reading the future in the hand is sometimes called *cheiromancy.* These words do not matter, but some people think they sound more scientific than 'hand-reading' or 'palmistry'.

Hand-watching

Hands can teach you a great deal about people without any formal reading. When you are with others, watch what they do with their hands, and read the obvious messages.

Palmists gain a lot of information from hands long before they start looking at the lines and mounts. Some people wave them about all the time, extrovertly. Some people make frequent nervous gestures. Some people are forever wringing or washing their hands – they may be nervous, or quick-thinking. Some thrust them in their pockets, out of sight. Hidden hands may indicate good listeners, but perhaps people who too easily change their minds.

Some people sit on their hands. Some hold them behind their backs, or fold them. Some plonk them aggressively on the hips. Some keep them relaxed or loose, and stab at the air with firm positive gestures. Clenched hands may show rage, or may indicate a restless and forceful personality. Just try some hand-watching in the bus, in the shops, in class, and you will be surprised how much you will begin to notice about people you don't know – and also about your friends.

There are many books about hand-reading, packed with detailed information and instructions. Here we provide only some simple suggestions, just to get you going.

How to Read Hands

You can read someone's hand almost anywhere, but the best place is sitting down facing the other person across a small table.

Always start by asking the other person whether he or she would like to have a reading; never force it on anyone. Warn them that you are not an expert; so they should not take what you say too seriously.

The other person will often offer you the right hand, palm up, because that is what they expect you to be interested in. You may find it worth having a quick look, to be polite, but then take both hands and lay them on the table palms down. They should be loose and relaxed, and not pressed down hard.

Take your time. Look at the hands for a few seconds, then touch them, move them –feel their weight. Feel the fingers, and bend one or two a little, to make sure they are relaxed. Preferably don't say anything yet. Begin to *form* your impressions, and check them off in your head against the list in the table on pages 191–4.

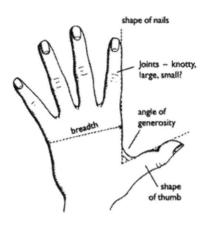

Figure 9.2: The shape and size of the hand is most revealing.

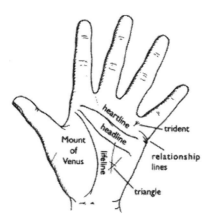

Figure 9.3: The palm of the hand, showing the most important mounts and lines.

Here are the 10 most fundamental things to look at – five from the backs of the hands, and five from the palms. *You should commit at least some of this table* to *memory before you start!*

Note that the three lines mentioned here – the Lifeline, the Headline and the Heartline – are clear to see on most hands. If the hand you are looking at does not seem to have one of them, don't worry. You will merely have to do your reading from the rest of the evidence.

1 Size	large hands	thoughtful, reflective, good with details but needs time to think
	broad hands	good mixer, enjoys work and play
	small hands	quick-thinking, a master-planner
	1st finger longer than 3rd	success
K	long little finger (beyond 2nd joint of 3rd finger)	skilled story-teller, successful writer or actor, perhaps teacher or academic

2 Shape	square hands	sensible, practical, helpful, hard-working
	Long, pointed hands	emotional, perhaps artistic, even psychic
	widely-spaced fingers	independent
	large knotty joints	logical, thoughtful – teacher, writer
C	long fingers	sensitive
	pointed fingertips	imaginative
3 Nail	long	tender spirit
	wide	outspoken, perhaps quarrelsome
	wedge-shaped	sensitive
	square	practical
	fluted	nervous
A	almond-shaped	possible psychic potential
4 Thumbs	large	strong personality
	broad	temperamental
	long	intelligent, strong will, born leader
	short	impressionable
B	stiff	stubborn
	waisted	tactful, sympathetic, loving, studious
5 Angle of generosity	1O°-30°	tendency to be mean
	30°-50°	generous
	50°-80°	open-handed, may even be too generous for your own good

6 Lifeline	*long, clear, curved down to wrist*	vitality and energy; the length does not necessarily indicate life-span
	curves round thumb	wonderful love life
	forked	travel, may spend part of life abroad
	breaks, crossings	may indicate illnesses, worries, danger
M	*crossings above thumb*	childhood illnesses
7 Headline	*long*	intelligent *(across to edge* = genius)
	straight across	logical, direct
	short + up-curve	possibly a scatterbrain
	long + up-curve	good memory (curve *at end* = money)
	gentle down curve	intuitive, imaginative, acting/music gift
	starts touching heartline	prudent, sensible, constructive
L	*starts well below heartline*	lively, uninhibited, lover of adventure
8 heartline	*longer than h'dline*	emotion controls logic
	shorter"	logic control emotion
A	*curved, long fork below finger*	warm, affectionate, romantic fortunate fork – luck & happiness in love
9 mount of venus	*well-developed*	love, sympathy, passion
	large near wrist	passionate, abundant energy, sexuality
	large near thumb	emotional
P	*large cross*	happy relationship
	criss-cross lines	passionate nature

10 special signs	*small horizontal line(s) below little finger*	marriage(s) or stable relationship(s) – the latest is nearest the finger
	small vertical lines meeting these	children from those relationships
	triangles, tripods, tridents	lucky, special abilities, tremendous ingenuity, perhaps a brilliant career.

How Does it Work?

Palmists may tell you there is magic in the hands. A traditional magic principle is 'As Above, So Below'. That is, by some magical power tedious things happening here on earth are a reflection of grander things happening in heaven. So it is, the theory goes, that we can read the future – or our destinies – in something as mundane as the lines of our hands.

Many magical ideas involve symbols, such as the simple pentagram or five-pointed star. Some palmists claim that the form of the mystic pentagram can be seen in the hand, and in the whole body. So what is happening in your body is reflected in the lines and shapes of your hands.

According to science, this has no foundation. Future events are unknown; they cannot directly affect your hands. No magical mechanisms are known that can convey ideas from 'above'. However, there are lots of ways in which palmistry might work, even if there is nothing magical about it.

Hands and Bodies

Obviously your hands will to some extent reflect your whole body – big people tend to have big hands, for example, and thin people have thin hands – and you may have noticed that there is nothing 'magical' about some of the suggestions we made about hand-watching. Nervous gestures reflect a nervous person; neat, clean hands and nails reflect a tidy, well-groomed person, while lots of nail polish probably indicates someone who wants to put on a good display, and perhaps hide her natural appearance.

At the other extreme, dirty hands reflect either a keen gardener, a mechanic, or a slovenly person – and you ought to be able to tell the difference with a quick look at their hair and clothes. None of this is magic, but you do need practice to begin to notice such things, and many unobservant people are terribly impressed when you can tell them the obvious in this way.

Most people are interested in their state of health, especially if there is anything wrong with them. Take a good look at the skin of the hands. You ought to be able to tell a good deal about the person's state of health. Are the hands pink and fresh-looking, or is the skin dull and tired?

Figure 9.4: Are the same patterns reflected in your body, your hand and the mystic pentagram?

Are there any cuts or scratches? In a healthy person any cuts will show signs of healing quickly and cleanly. In an unhealthy person a simple cut may look reddened or sore.

You might say something like, 'You are feeling a little run-down at the moment. Your back sometimes aches a little.' In fact most adults suffer from backache at some time in their lives and this is more likely to happen when they are run-down or ill in some other way. Yet they can still be tremendously impressed if you mention it when they thought no one knew! Furthermore, they may well be grateful to have a genuine chance to talk about their problems.

Other Clues

A wedding ring gives you a simple piece of evidence to work from. Don't waste it by saying, 'Ah – I see you are married.' Try something a little more adventurous (but still likely enough to succeed) like, 'You have had some ups and down in your marriage' (who hasn't?) 'but you realize it is worth trying your best to make your relationships work.'

Don't just look at the hands. As you become a skilled reader you will use every little clue to your advantage. If your client is carrying a book, weave that into your observations. Stroking one finger, you might say, 'I see you have lots of books at home' or 'I get the impression you are interested in history.'

Look for other things the person is carrying, such as car keys or a bicycle helmet, shopping or a briefcase. Note what shops any carrier bag came from, or any travel tags on a case or handbag.

You will soon realize that not every comment has to be spot on. People tend to be amazed by the things palm-readers get right, and forget most of the ones they get wrong. So you can afford to stick out your neck a little and go beyond what you are completely sure about. The great advantage of going for the details is that you may well score one or two spectacular hits.

> Sherlock Holmes … shook his head with a smile as he noticed my questioning glances. 'Beyond the obvious facts that he has at some time done manual labour, that he takes snuff, that he is a Freemason, that he has been in China, and that he has done a considerable amount of writing lately, I can deduce nothing else.'
>
> Mr Jabez Wilson started up in his chair … 'How in the name of good fortune did you know all that, Mr Holmes?' he asked …
>
> 'Your hands, my dear sir. Your right hand is quite a size larger than your left. You have worked with it, and the muscles are more developed.'
>
> … 'Ah, of course, I forgot that. But the writing?'
>
> 'What else can be indicated by that right cuff so very shiny for five inches, and the left one with the smooth patch near the elbow where you rest it upon the desk?'
>
> 'Well, but China?'
>
> 'The fish which you have tattooed immediately above your right wrist could only have been done in China …'
>
> (The *Redheaded League,* Sir Arthur Conan Doyle)

I love reading Sherlock Holmes stories – even 100 years on they are thoroughly enjoyable. Yet two things always disappoint me slightly. First, we are never told about the shiny cuff, the tattoo and so on, until after Holmes has made his deductions – so we don't have a chance to test our own skills of observation. Second, I don't think I have ever met anyone with a fish tattooed above the right wrist, let alone all the other things that Holmes' clients seem to be smothered with. Nevertheless, Sherlock Holmes was the 'master of deduction' and the logical way in which he progresses from observation to deduction is a joy.

Holmes used to say to Dr Watson, 'You see, but you do not observe!' If you want to become an impressive handreader, you need to learn how to observe.

Cold Reading

All these clues are commonly used by magicians in what they call 'cold reading' – and by magicians I mean stage magicians, conjurors or tricksters – not the sort who perform rituals and cast spells. Magic shows often include demonstrations of 'mind-reading' that are actually done using some simple psychological tricks.

One such trick is to 'read' a person's mind from his or her reactions. Palmistry is an excellent way to do this because you have hold of the person's hand. You can actually feel his or her reactions directly.

Take a simple example. You hold the person's hand and run your finger along the headline saying – rather slowly, as though you are thinking deeply 'Now, this is the headline. Here are indications of … um … how you use your intelligence and … er … also of musical ability and the imagination.' As you say this you should appear to be studying the line, but in fact you should be feeling the person's reaction to each word. If on the word 'music' she moves towards you, tenses, looks up and generally appears alert, then she is interested. Look at the tips of those left-hand fingers: are they toughened by frequent pressing on guitar or violin strings? While you are looking, take that word 'music' and play with it; move the conversation one stage further: 'You are interested in music. Do you play an instrument? Perhaps a stringed instrument?'

A question like this is probably enough. The surprised client will say, 'Why yes, I play the violin. I've just started to learn,' and may even go away convinced that you told her that she played the violin. If the answer is 'No', you can try asking whether she enjoys listening to music, or try the line, 'Well, you may have some undeveloped musical potential.' People love to be told they have hidden depths.

One of the oddest things is that people who go to clairvoyants and palmists often think that the palmist told *them* everything when in fact the palmist asked a lot of questions and just repeated back what was said to him or her. So if you want to practise being a palmist let your 'clients' talk as much as they want, and listen carefully. Feed it all back in a slightly different way, and you may be taken for a palm-reading genius.

If the person reacts to none of the aspects of the headline, go on to the heartline. Again, watch for any reaction. If you get a big one here you will know that he is concerned about an affair of the heart. If you simply say 'I can see in this line that you are worried about a relationship' you may suddenly find you have made an impression. Before you know it you have a person who really does think you know his mind. When you then come up with some generalities about trouble with relationships you will be well away. If you can improve your remarks by tailoring them to the person's age and sex, you will do even better.

All this sounds simple. In a way it is. Psychologists have done many experiments to show how easily people are fooled by personality readings. But trainee palm-readers need some practice to get their skills right. The experiments that have been done also show that the effect is most convincing when the reader appears to be relaxed and confident, and when he or she makes it appear that the reading is 'especially for you'. Palmistry is good for this because you are reading people's own hands. It really does seem as though it is specially for them.

The Right Motivation

Palmistry may work through the magic of the hands or through the mystery of psychology, but whichever you think is true you should ask yourself, 'Why am I doing this?' If your answer is to impress people or to gain power over them, then don't do it. You may merely be after a bit of fun at a party and that's OK. Or if your motivation is to help people, your newly developing skills may be really valuable. Any insight you can give people into their own personality may help them to understand themselves, and nothing is more helpful to worried people than a chance to talk freely about themselves in an atmosphere of caring.

Some Sensible Precautions

If you have started to learn how to read hands, you will probably be surprised at how effectively you achieve results. You may also be surprised at how keen people can be to have a palm-reader to call on. The reason is simply that everyone wants to learn about themselves.

Once your friends learn that you read palms, you may even get asked to do it for a school or village fete, at a party, or for someone's birthday treat. There are a number of sensible precautions to think about if you want to do this.

First, protect yourself. Do not make false or ridiculous claims. Indeed it is far better to state at the beginning that you are only a beginner and that you are doing it only for fun. In other words, make sure you don't mislead people.

Don't take any money for your services. Professional readers often claim that the occult arts will not work when done for a profit. This may or may not be true, but psychologically there is all the difference in the world between doing something for fun or to help someone, and doing it for personal gain. If you refuse to take any money you will not be tempted to exploit people; nor will you be giving them false expectations – or reason to complain if your reading is not too brilliant.

This does not preclude doing something for charity. As long as you stress that you are not an expert you might well charge a small fee to give to saving dolphins, rebuilding the church roof, or helping children in trouble. If you go about this the right way it can be fun and even helpful to people.

Second, protect your 'clients', too. There are some real dangers in any kind of divination, whether it is psychic reading, palmistry, Tarot or tea-leaf reading. People can take what you tell them far too seriously. So do not tell them anything that is likely to be disturbing or frightening.

If you ever become a real expert, or have training in counselling, you might be able to judge what it is safe or helpful to say. As a beginner just stay right away from dangerous topics like when someone is going to die or what diseases he or she will have. Do not tell young women that they will never have children, nor that they will be pregnant next week, and avoid the uncertainties that can really worry people such as whether they will pass their exams or driving test. Learn some evasive tactics in case people try to push you to give an answer. 'I cannot see this little wrinkle clearly enough' might do, or 'The future lies in your own hands. Take care to do your best.'

One more danger to watch out for – if you practise and get good at reading hands you may start to convince yourself that palmistry really works – that it is indeed a magical way of finding out about people. But could it all be just psychology? The only way to find out for sure is to do some experiments yourself.

Palmistry Experiments

If you have the opportunity to do lots of readings for your friends or acquaintances you might try to vary the procedure and see whether it makes any difference. For example, you could swap round two lines. Call the headline the heartline and vice versa. Do your clients notice any difference?

Ray Hyman, a well-known psychologist, once learned to read palms and got such positive comments from the people whose hands he read that he was convinced he had learned an occult skill. A sceptical friend then suggested that he tried saying the opposite to everything he saw in the lines and mounts of the hand. When he discovered that his clients were just as happy with this, he changed his mind about his own powers. Indeed, he went on to write books about the ways in which people can be fooled.

If the magical theories about palmistry are correct, then all the information you need for a reading is actually in the hand. However, if it is all psychology there is more information in the rest of the person and in the interaction between the two of you than there is in the hand itself. Can you think of ways to find out which is true?

One way is to isolate the hand from the rest of the person (and not by cutting it off!) A fun way to do this is to put up some kind of screen with a hole in it. You can drape a cloth or sheet over a blackboard or flip chart stand, or you can make a support out of a couple of chairs on top of a table. If you have an old sheet you can cut a hand-sized hole in it. If you don't want to do that, arrange two cloths so that a hand can easily be slipped between them.

Once your screen is ready you need to get someone to sit the other side and put his or her hand through... but obviously you must not know who it is. Either get a friend to bring along someone you don't know, or play this as a party game – divide into two groups, and for each session one group provides the sitter and the other the palmist. Ask the sitter to put his or her hand through the hole but to say nothing at all. Now see how you get on reading the hand.

Can you think why this test not foolproof? In fact the palm-reader still has quite a lot of psychological information to go on, especially if he or she is allowed to touch the hand.

You might decide to allow the palm-reader only to look at the hand, and not touch it. This will reduce the clues available, but there will still be some. For example, if the person is very worried about an exam or test, you may actually see a slight tensing of the wrist and fingers when you mention the subject – and the reader is away. So this is a fun party game, but it does not really rule out enough of the normal explanations to be a good scientific test. Somehow you need to be able to see the hand without having any contact with the person.

Photocopied Hands

Before the invention of photocopiers, palmists used to make handprints with large ink pads and absorbent paper. This was messy, and quite tricky to get right. The frequent result was ink all over the furniture and the poor client's clothes. Fortunately all you need to do with a modern photocopier is place your hand on top of the glass and press 'start'. But do watch out that you don't make a mess of the glass. Ensure your hand is clean and dry before you do it (and if you do leave a horrible sweaty handprint, wipe the glass thoroughly with a cloth).

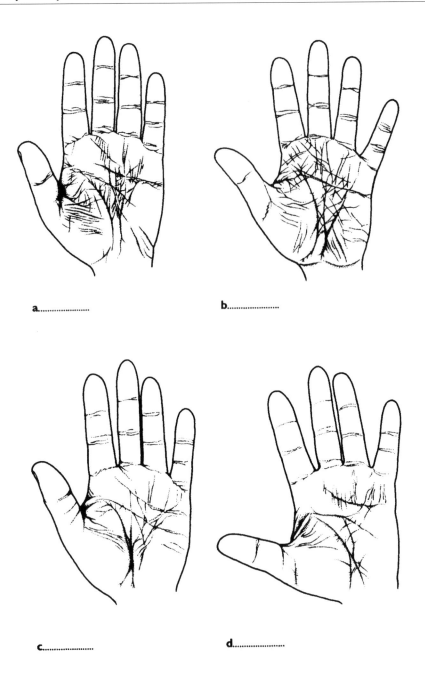

Figure 9.5: These men's handprints were made by: an actor on stage and television a nurse, a baker, and an author of this book. Can you work out which is which? Write your answers below –or on a separate sheet of paper. (Answers on page 211.)

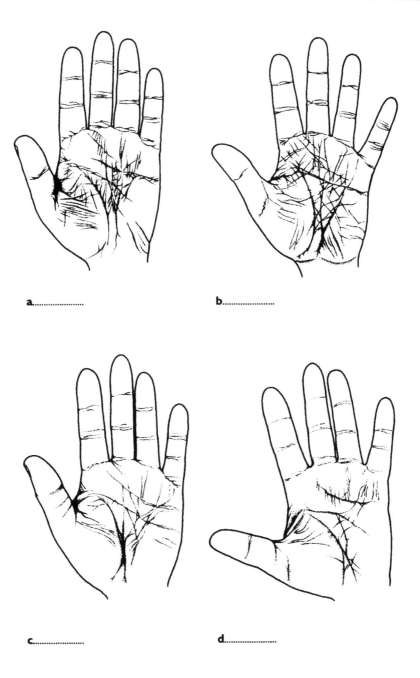

Figure 9.6: These four women's handprints were made by a famous mathematician, a hairdresser, a teacher, and an author of this book. Can you work out which is which? Write your answers below –or on a separate sheet of paper. (Answers on page 211.)

Don't press on the glass, just rest your hand gently on it. We suggest you don't put the cover down, and set the copier for two points darker than normal on the light/dark scale, otherwise the hand may come out plain white against a black background. However, photocopiers vary; so if possible try out several settings. What you want is a clear, sharp image, with nothing bleached-out white, and all the main lines of the palm clear.

Now you have a method of making handprints, can you design an experiment to test whether palmistry is all psychology or really magic?

Here is one you can try without any preparation at all. It will also give you some useful practice if you want to try a more elaborate experiment yourself.

On pages 204 and 205 are eight handprints. We have chosen these to be as different as possible, so that if palmistry really works you should be able to work out which is which. Women's hands are usually smaller than men's. So we have given you four men's hands and four women's. They are all reduced in the photocopy by an equal amount.

Study them carefully. You can see the shape of the hands and all the lines clearly. Working from what you have learned, can you deduce who is who? Use the information in the palmistry table on pages 191–96. For example, teachers and writers are supposed to have long little fingers and large knotty joints. Artists are supposed to have long, pointed hands. Which professions would you associate with more emotion than logic (a longer heartline) or the opposite (a longer headline)? If palmistry works, you should be able to identify them all.

Write down your answers, either in the space provided or on a piece of paper, before you look at the correct answers on page 211.

Controlled Experiments

How did you get on with the hands provided? You can now adapt this method to use people of your own choosing and find out whether palmistry really works.

The principle of this experiment is to find out whether the information in a handprint can tell you about the person whose hand it is. In the previous experiment you had only the occupation of the person to go on, and this may or may not be enough. You might be able to do better if you could find out more details about the person, especially those details that are supposed to be related to the lines and mounts of their palms.

This is easy if you know the people well, but then there is a big problem. If you know them well you probably know something about their hands. You will have shaken their hands, held them, or just looked at them, and you may be able to tell whose is whose – even subconsciously. So you need a way to find out about the people who are not already friends of yours.

One way is to use a questionnaire. We have designed a simple one you can use. This simply asks about eight points that are supposed to be important in palmistry. If you prefer, you can make up your own. You might think that other details are important, or you may want to add additional ones.

What You Need

- 2 Experimenters, one to be Palm-reader and one to be Assistant.
- 4 people to have their hands read.
- 4 copies of the palmistry questionnaire, numbered 1–4.
- Palmistry Record Sheets.

Palmistry Questionnaire

Here are eight statements that might apply to you. Please say how true they are of you by putting a circle round the appropriate number. For example, ring 'I' if you strongly agree, '4' if you disagree but not very strongly, or '3' if you neither agree nor disagree. Remember, there are no right answers. We want to find out about you.

1. For *me, emotion is more important than logic.*
Strongly agree   1   2   3   4   5   Strongly disagree

2. *I am extremely intelligent.*
Strongly agree   1   2   3   4   5   Strongly disagree

3. *I am imaginative and artistic.*
Strongly agree   1   2   3   4   5   Strongly disagree

4. *I have a tendency to be mean.*
Strongly agree   1   2   3   4   5   Strongly disagree

5. *I am full of vitality and energy.*
Strongly agree   1   2   3   4   5   Strongly disagree

6. *I have an excellent memory.*
Strongly agree   1   2   3   4   5   Strongly disagree

7. *I am warm, affectionate, and romantic.*
Strongly agree   1   2   3   4   5   Strongly disagree

8. *I am driven by logic more than by emotion.*
Strongly agree   1   2   3   4   5   Strongly disagree

Procedure

The *Assistant's* job is most important and must be done carefully.

You will need to make sure the Palm-reader cannot know which prints go with which questionnaire. You should label each handprint with a letter, A–D. To decide which letters to use you need a random process. You might like to put four pieces of paper with letters A–D on them into a hat or small container. For person number one pull out a letter (say it's C). Make yourself a secret Assistant's List 1 = C, 2 = A, and so on.

Find four people who are all rather different from each other, and ask them if they would mind having their hands photocopied and filling in a brief questionnaire. If they agree, carefully make a photocopy of each person's left hand. (Do both hands if you wish, but the left should be enough.) Try to ensure that they just rest the hand gently on the glass and do not press down. Check that all the photocopies are of similar quality. Label the first person's handprint C, the second A, and so on, according to your list.

Make four copies of the questionnaire, number them, and give one to each person, asking them to fill it in. Take your 'Assistant's List' and fill in each person's name next to the number of the questionnaire you have given them. The subjects have now done their part of the experiment. You should have a handprint and a questionnaire from each person.

You now have the key list. *Do not* show this list to the Palm-reader until the end of the experiment. Keep it in a safe place and don't tell anyone what's on it. You must be especially careful not to give away any clues to the Palm-reader.

Now give the questionnaires and handprints to the Palm-reader.

Palmistry record sheet – Assistant's list

Questionnaire Number	Name	Hand Prints Letter (A–D)
1		
2		
3		
4		

The *Palm-reader* should take all the photocopies of the hand-prints and study them carefully. The questionnaires will tell you some crucial facts about each person. Using the palmistry table *(pages 190–96)* you should now be able to match up the handprints to the questionnaires. Take the Palmist's Record Sheet and fill in your guess as to which goes with which. When you have completed this Record sheet – *but not before* – you can ask your Assistant for key list.

Palmistry record sheet – Palmist's list

Questionnaire Number	Palmist's Guess (A–D)	Correct Answer (A–D)	Tick if Correct
1			
2			
3			
4			

Total Correct _____

The Results

Fill in the number of correct matches on your record sheet. How did you do? On the basis of your results do you think that palmistry really works? And if it does, does it work by magic or by psychology?

Further Experiments

You may have found problems with this experiment. For example, matching the questionnaires with the handprints can be seriously difficult. Perhaps you decided to use only questions 1 and 8, and to look only at the head and heartlines. You could design a new, simpler experiment this way if you like.

You might also devise your own experiments based on other characteristics. For example, could you test whether the angle of generosity really is related to how mean someone is? You might wonder whether people would be honest about this. Should you watch their behaviour rather than just have them fill in the question on a questionnaire? This seems a good idea – but how? Or could you ask their friends to tell you how generous they are?

Love and relationships are supposed to be visible in the hands. Do adult hands tell you about the number of marriages, love affairs, or children? If palmistry really works the way its adherents claim, all these things should make good experiments – and give positive results. There is no limit to the ways you could devise to find out.

Palmistry Experiment – Correct answers

Men's prints: **A** Baker **B** Actor of stage and television **C** Nurse **D** Author

Women's prints: **A** Author **B** Hairdresser **C** Teacher **D** Famous Mathemarician

10

Astrology

A thousand years ago there were no books, no television, no radio, no electricity. When the weather was not too miserable, millions of people must have sat out in the open at night and looked up at the only form of natural entertainment there was – above their heads.

Today most of us scarcely notice the stars, but if you take the trouble to stay out and watch them for even a few hours, you can easily begin to be captivated by their patterns, their predictability, their sheer numbers and the majesty of their solemn cartwheeling march across the great darkness of the night sky.

Within hours you begin to notice the movement – the way they climb slowly from the eastern horizon in a fixed order, but in a procession that changes slowly with the weeks and months.

Details of what to expect in the heavens are printed in some newspapers on about the last day of each month, for the following month. Thus on about 30 or 31 August you will find a section about 'the night sky in September'. The first things you see, if you wait outside as darkness falls, are often planets. Venus and Jupiter are frequently brighter than anything else in the sky; so they show up first in the evening. Mars and Saturn can be picked out from the stars too, and

Mercury (if it isn't hidden by the sun) can be impressively bright.

Above all the Moon dominates the dark sky, with its varying shape and intense brightness.

Imagine watching this silent pageant, night after night, instead of the television. We should hardly be surprised that the ancient watchers imagined in the sky the figures of their gods and heroes, their monsters, beasts and friends. There are so many stars you can join the dots in as many ways as you like, but we have inherited a set of 'constellations' perhaps from the Egyptians or the Babylonians.

Ursa *major,* the Great Bear, looks more like a saucepan to me – and indeed Americans call it 'the Big Dipper'. But the constellation is easy to recognize, and it's useful because the last two stars, the 'pointers', point almost directly at the pole star – so you can tell which way is north, without a compass.

One of the simplest tenets of magical belief was – and is – 'As above, so below,' and what could be more satisfying than to try to link the drama continually being played out in the heavens with that on Earth. Surely we down here, and our lives and loves and futures, must be reflected in the sky?

Why Study the Stars?

There is in us a natural wish to know what is going to happen. We would quite like to know whether rain will fall tomorrow; we should definitely want to know if a natural disaster – a flood or storm or fire – were imminent. And most of all, we want to know about ourselves and own destinies.

We are less interested in reports of the past – who cares whether it rained yesterday? That's why we have weather forecasts on television, even though they usually seem to be wrong. We would rather have a poor forecast than none at all.

So with ourselves; we want to know our future – and if that is uncertain, then we should like to know about our inner selves – are we deep down generous and kind-hearted, or born leaders? Have we hidden musical and artistic talents, along with a sensitive soul? If we cannot find out our futures, let us try to discover our true present selves.

Whatever the reasons, many people do seem to believe that the stars have influence on our lives. Sometimes in the West we scoff at the people of other cultures who choose their partners with much astrological help – but a great many Westerners look at their horoscopes on the way to work in the morning, and a poll among American teenagers in 1983 showed that more than half of them believed that astrology works.

According to popular legend, while Ronald Reagan was President of the US his wife Nancy employed a personal astrologer, and since she was supposed frequently to advise the President, there was the image of the US government apparently being directed by astrology.

The brilliant astronomer Tycho Brahe discovered a new comet in 1577, but although he was one of the founders of modern astronomy and cosmology, he used the comet as the basis of an *astrological* prediction that a prince would be born in Finland and become King of Sweden, invade Germany, and die in 1632 – which was exactly what Gustavus Adolphus did.

The Complexity of Astrology

To most ordinary people, astrology is simply the sun signs listed in the newspapers and magazines. You know your sun sign, and look up your horoscope. In reality, the art is far more complex.

The basic theory is that your character and therefore your future are influenced by the positions of heavenly bodies at the time of your birth. A baby born at a particular moment is supposed to partake of the nature of that moment, which in turn is supposed to be determined by the positions of the Sun, the Moon and the planets within the zodiac of the 12 constellations. The map of the moment, or horoscope, is a representation of those positions, and therefore the astrologer's chief tool in determining the nature of a person.

The crudest measure is the sun sign, which is essentially a statement of which month includes your birthday. As the Earth revolves around the Sun, during the course of the year, the Sun seems to move across the background of the stars, and so appears within each of the 12 major constellations for about a month. The Sun is in Capricorn on 1st January; in Aquarius on 1st February, and so on.

However, the planets also move across the background of the stars, and they too are supposed to influence us. Mars is red, and stands for the god of war, courage and aggression. Venus, looking white and soft, was the goddess of love and beauty – even though we now know those soft white clouds are made mainly of sulphuric acid!

The planets move in a predictable but complex way, and there are eight of them (other than the Earth) to take into consideration. Since they all interact with each other, and the angles between them are often reckoned to be important, there is plenty of scope for variation. Furthermore, the positions of all these bodies change continuously, so the time of your birth down to the exact hour and minute, and whereabouts on Earth you were born, are often said to be crucial.

Until recently, the casting of a precise horoscope was a long and tedious business. The astrologer had to do many calculations and consult a special book of tables, called an *Ephemeris,* to work out just where all the planets were at any particular time. All this took a lot of time and hard work, and created much mystique. The sheer complexity may help to explain why in the West one person in every 10,000 practises or studies serious astrology – far more than practise serious astronomy.

Nowadays the calculations can easily be done by computer. Indeed, this is just the sort of thing computers are good at. Arguably the astrologer still has to do the more interesting part – working out what the horoscope means. Nevertheless, a great change has occurred, since getting your horoscope calculated means only pressing a couple of buttons. You can spend a lot of money sending away for a computer horoscope, and you might like to consider just what the owner of the computer has to do for that money.

What Do Horoscopes Tell Us?

The most important single influence on us is supposed to come from the Sun. Over the page are some of the characteristics attributed to people with each of the 12 Sun signs.

			best partners in	
sign	characteristics	good at these jobs	business	love
Aries ram 21 Mar-20 Apr	keen, creative, enthusiastic, energetic, hot-headed, quick to anger, humorous, quick-witted, assertive, natural leaders	surgeons, racing drivers, athletes, salespeople, estate agents, soldiers	Aq, Pis, Tau, Sag	Ar, Gem, Leo, Lib, Sag

Taurus bull 21 Apr- 20 May	cautious, patient, practical, often remarkable memory, well-liked, generous, strong, good at sports, music, money	accountants, builders, chemists, engineers, gardeners, teachers, photographers	Ar, Gem, Pis, Sco	Cap, Lib, Sco, Vir
Gemini twins 21 May– 20 June	adaptable, affectionate, generous, clever, witty, imaginative, intellectual, positive, communicative	travel agents, sales, couriers, advertising, television, transport, teachers, politicians	Tau, Lib, Sag, Can	Lib, Aq, Ar, Leo, Sag
Cancer *crab* 21 June- 20 July	traditionalists, active – enjoy travel/adventure; sensitive, imaginative, affectionate, but may not show these things	scientists, caterers, politicians, teachers, manufacturers, artists, librarians, nurses	Aq, Cap, Gem, Leo	Cap, Pis, Sco, Lib
Leo *lion* 21 July- 21 Aug	exuberant, energetic, positive, born leaders, ambitious, brave, idealistic, impulsive, generous, loyal, vital, powerful	managers, hoteliers, doctors, nurses, actors, estate agents, sales executives	all, but esp. Can, Vir, Aq	Aq, Ar, Can, Leo, Sag, Vir
Virgo *virgin* 22 Aug- 22 Sep	inquiring, intuitive, analytical, alert, hard- working, tolerant but fearful of illness, pain, accidents, financial problems	social workers, craftworkers, writers, lawyers, professors, architects, designers	Leo, Pis, Sco, Vir	Ar, Cap, Pis, Tau, Vir

Libra *scales* 23 Sep– 22 Oct	sympathetic, understanding, intuitive, clear-thinking, susceptible, strong-minded, original, far-sighted, shrewd	hairdressers, valuers, speculators, actors, inventors, jewellers, beauticians, singers	Gem, Sco, Vir	Aq, Ar, Gem, Leo, Sag, Sco
Scorpio *scorpion* 23 Oct– 22 Nov	quiet, observant, analytical, self-confident, aggressive, loyal friends, passionate lovers, cool under fire	detectives, police, psychiatrists, doctors, branch managers, chiefs of industry	Can, Lib, Sag, Vir, Tau	Can, Leo, Pis, Tau, Vir
Sagit-tarius *bowman* 23 Nov– 20 Dec	active, cheerful, focused, penetrating mind, workers not seekers, versatile, outspoken, impulsive, neat, methodical	travellers, sailors, bankers, airline pilots financiers, farmers, working with horses	Ar, Cap, Gem, Leo, Sco	Ar, Gem, Leo, Lib. Sag
Capri-corn *goat* 21 Dec– 19 Jan	scholarly, intellectual, thinkers, philosophers, calm, deliberate, loners, practical, but may have psychic ability	politicians, managers, financiers, builders, accountants, teachers, lecturers, lawyers	Aq, Can, Sag, Tau, Vir	Ar, Tau, Vir
Aquarius *water-carrier* 20 Jan– 18 Feb	simple, unassuming, original, loners, active, volatile, famous people who rise from obscurity, humanitarians	astronauts, scientists, musicians, poets, politicians, pioneers, auctioneers, lawyers	Ar, Gem, Lib, Pis	Gem, Leo, Lib

Pisces *fish* 19 Feb– 20 Mar	unselfish, doubters, sometimes unachievers, sincere, devoted, good lovers, trustworthy, calm, jovial, determined	dancers, government employees, scientists, engineers, sailors, environme- ntalists	Aq, Ar, Cap, Tau Vir	Can, Sco, Vir

Does Astrology Work?

One intriguing fact is that there are many books on astrology. Each lists the characteristics of people with particular signs, like those above, and they all differ, if only slightly. They cannot all be right, if they are all different. Also, it seems inconceivable that everyone born under, say, Aries, would have the same personality and the same kind of life. So is astrology nonsense?

There are many daily newspapers and weekly magazines that carry horoscopes. If horoscopes were true, then many of the predictions for particular signs would be the same – but they aren't. Indeed, the magazines vary considerably in what they say, although they provide more advice than prediction – 'You should watch out for unexpected danger on the road this week,' which applies to most people most weeks and is therefore an easy way out for the writer.

Astrologers say that sun-sign astrology is too simple; to be accurate you need a really precise birth chart. This means having your complete horoscope drawn up for the moment at which you were born. The astrologers argue that sun signs give the general picture, but only the full horoscope gives a personal, unique picture of *you*.

Experiments have been done to test this claim. Between 1978 and 1986, seven studies were made of birth charts in which a total of 230 people were invited to choose which of two (or more) birth chart interpretations best fitted their real characteristics. In each case one of the birth charts was their own, the others incorrect. The results showed that people would have done slightly better just by guessing than they did by trying to pick out their own characteristics.

In 1950 the French statistician Michel Gauquelin set out to disprove some of the claims of astrologers, and found to his surprise that although the claims he was attacking were indeed false, there were some statistical anomalies in his results. He examined and refined them, and found to his own amazement that for certain groups of highly successful people there was a significant correlation between their profession and the arrangement of the planets at their birth.

He discovered that top scientists were more likely to be born with Saturn on the ascendant or one of the angles, while for successful soldiers and athletes the equivalent planet was likely to be Mars. The odds were millions to one against this having happened by chance.

This finding, the so called 'Gauquelin Effect', has been successfully replicated and appears to be genuine. It is a real mystery! However, it is a very odd effect and not one of the classic mainstays of traditional astrology. What is often forgotten is that Gauquelin searched for many, many correlations and failed to find them. Although he did some of the best research on astrology, most of his results were negative. In 1969, in his book *The Scientific Basis for Astrology*, Gauquelin wrote:

> It is now quite certain that the signs in the sky which presided over our births have no power whatever to decide our fates, to affect our hereditary characteristics,

or to play any part, however humble, in the totality of effects, random or otherwise, which form the fabric of our lives and mould our impulses to actions.

So, while claiming a peculiar anomaly, he still rejected the idea of horoscopes predicting personality. However, he did point out that a fundamental tenet of astrology remains true – we are all interconnected and we do not understand all the links between ourselves and the rest of the universe.

Possible Mechanism for Influence from the Heavens

Dr Frank Brown from Northwestern University, noting that oysters open and close their shells in time with the tides, wondered whether the oysters were prompted by the actual rise and fall of the sea, or by the varying influence of the Moon. After all, the tides in the sea are caused mainly by the Moon. So he took some oysters from the Atlantic and moved them in dark containers to Evanston, Illinois, 1,000 miles from the ocean.

Within two weeks the oysters were opening and closing their shells in time not with the tide on their native shore, but with what the tide would have been if the ocean had come to Evanston. In other words, the oysters seemed to be influenced by the Moon, rather than by the water level. He went on to show that the Moon seemed to have some influence on rats and beans and potatoes, too.

So it seems that the Moon may be able to effect changes on Earth – but how it does so is not clear. The tides are caused by the gravitational pull of the Moon, but they are noticeable only because there is an immense volume of water available in the ocean. The midwife attending the expectant mother has a much greater influence on a child about to be born than does the Moon. Most of the planets are bigger than the Moon, but they are all much further away, and the gravitational effect on the baby being born would be less from any planet than from a mosquito on the midwife's shoulder.

From the point of view of physics and astronomy it seems impossible that astrology could work – yet many millions of people believe that it does. It is probably the most popular of the occult arts. Thousands of people practise astrology, and millions consult these astrologers. A great deal of money is made by newspapers, booksellers and computer software sellers, not to mention the astrologers themselves. There must be something in it. But is that something written in the stars or in our own minds? We need some experiments to find out.

Scientific Tests

Find a horoscope from an old magazine or newspaper – ideally last month's magazine or last week's newspaper – and look up your own sun sign. Is it amazingly true? Does it seem to describe things about you that no one else would know? Was it uncannily accurate in predicting what actually happened? It ought to be. If horoscopes did not manage this at least some of the time, they would not be in the back pages of so many magazines and most of the daily papers. Astrology columns make money. But why?

Perhaps astrology really works, and you and your life follow patterns laid out in your sun sign. If this is so, the only predictions that really fit you should be the ones for your own sun sign.

Look now at the predictions for the other sun signs. Are they just as good for you? If there is nothing whatever in astrology, then the predictions for the other 11 signs should fit you just as well as your own.

However, there is a problem here. You know which one is supposed to be yours and so you are biased when reading through them. To make a real scientific test you need to conceal from the readers which are the predictions intended for them. This can form the basis of a good experiment, and indeed it is the method that has been used in many scientific tests of astrology. You can do this experiment in a fun and informal way – almost as a party game. Or you can do it in a properly controlled way.

Experiment 1: A Party Game

The idea behind this experiment is to take all 12 forecasts from a magazine astrology column, mix them up, and then see whether your friends can pick their own from among all the others. You should do this at the end of the month, when all the events should have happened – if they were going to.

If astrology is all psychological, then people should do no better than chance in this test. If astrology works – by which we mean if the events predicted are specific to each sun sign – then people should easily be able to pick out their own, even if a few of the details are not correct.

What You Need

- An Experimenter
- Some friends to act as Subjects
- 2 copies of the astrological forecasts from a monthly magazine
- Results Sheet (see page 216)

Preparation

Take a copy of the astrological forecasts from a monthly magazine. Try to choose a magazine that your subjects are unlikely to have seen. It would spoil the experiment completely if they had read the forecasts before and remembered which was theirs!

The forecasts are usually in the form of a paragraph or so for each sun sign, outlining the main events and problems that the month will bring. You need to check that the forecasts themselves do not give away which sun sign they are about. For example, they might say 'This month even Leos may feel a little lonely around the 15th.' Avoid these, as it is difficult to cut the words out. Also, try to pick a magazine that gives as much specific information as possible. Some are vague, giving only advice, which would make it very difficult for your subjects to choose between them.

Buy a spare copy of the magazine, or copy the page, so that there is one copy for you and one for the Subjects. Keep your own copy safely hidden away.

Now cut out each of the horoscopes and cut off the sun signs, so that you just have the 12 forecasts and no indication of which belongs to which sign. Mix them all up and stick them on to a large sheet of card or thick paper to make a kind of poster. If you are really going to do this at a party you can then stick it up on the wall. Next to each forecast write one of the letters A–L, and underneath it leave a few spaces for people to write their names and sun signs in.

At the top of your sheet write some instructions for your friends who are going to take part. They might be something like the following:

Astrology Game

Do you believe in astrology? You can help try to prove it works!

All the forecasts below were taken from the horoscope section in last month's magazine.

Simply read them all and decide which best applies to you.

When you have chosen, please write your name and sun sign underneath it.

Good Luck.

Results

When all your friends have had a go and written down their answers, you can check the results. Take down the poster and write the correct sun signs against each of the letters (if you want to use the poster again you can write these on little sticky papers and take them off again when you've finished checking).

Now take the Results Sheet on page 216 and fill it in. Put down the name of each person, his or her own sun sign and the letter he or she chose. In the fourth column write down the sun sign associated with the letter chosen. If this is actually the persons's sun sign then he or she has got it right and you can tick the final column.

How many people chose the right forecast? If they were all independent then each person would have a 1-in-12 chance of getting it right, just by guessing. So how many must get it right for you to have a significant result?

Suppose you had just four people at your party. Then if two get it right, your result is significant.

Suppose now you have eight. When eight people guess, just at random, there's a 50:50 chance that one of them will get it right. So don't be surprised if one or two do pick the right one. In this case you need three people choosing correctly for a significant result.

In fact you can go up to 14 people at your party and if three get it right it will still be significant. If more than that get it right you are really doing well.

Astrology Results Sheet

	Name	Sun sign	Chosen letter	Chosen Sun sign	Tick if correct
1					
2					
3					
4					
5					

Total Correct _____

Did You Get a Significant Result?

No? This suggests that astrological forecasts are not very specific. If you can't pick your own out *after* the event, it would be pretty useless to depend on its predictions *beforehand.* It could be that all the apparent success of astrology is really just good psychology. There is nothing more to it than that.

Yes? If you did get a significant result, it shows that people are indeed able to pick out their own astrological forecasts from all the others. This might be evidence that astrology works – unless, that is, there are other reasons why they might have picked the right one.

To design a really scientific experiment you have to rule out all the other possibilities you can think of. So what else might have enabled them to choose the right one?

We have mentioned the problem that the subjects might have already seen the magazine you chose to use. Also, they were all doing it together. If even one had seen the magazine he or she might tell the others. Doing it together is also a problem, since the statistical test is valid only if all the choices are independent – and they won't be if people stand around discussing them. These are just a few reasons for wanting to do a properly controlled test.

Experiment 2: Controlled Test
The basic idea behind this experiment is just the same as the previous one. The only difference is in the procedure. Instead of putting the forecasts up on a board for all to see, this time you test each person individually.

Requirements
As above plus a quiet room in which to do the test. You should not know the sun signs of the people you are testing just in case you influence their choice.

Preparation
Cut out the astrological forecasts as before, only this time stick each one individually on a piece of thick paper or card and write a letter (A–L) on the back. If you want your experiment to be really foolproof you could get someone else to prepare the cards, so that you cannot possibly influence the choices made by knowing which forecast belongs to which sun sign. You should now have 12 cards, each with a forecast on one side and a letter on the other.

Procedure
Ideally you should have a table in a quiet room and ask each subject to come in alone. Lay out all 12 forecasts on the table

and ask the subject to read them all carefully. You might say something like this:

> Thank you for coming to take part in my experiment. I want you, please, to read all these 12 astrological forecasts. They are all taken from last month's issue of a magazine and are supposed to describe the main events, concerns and problems that you have had during the past month. Please read each one carefully and then tell me which one you think best describes your month.

Your subjects may well find it difficult to pick one, but encourage them to do so, even if they are unsure. Now turn over the card they have chosen, note the letter on the back, and write it down on the Results Sheet. After you have written down their choice (not before!), ask them their sun sign and enter this on the sheet as well. Thank your subject, and then do the same with the other subjects, until all of them have chosen their forecasts.

You may, if you like, do all the subjects in turn and complete the experiment in half an hour or so. Alternatively you can keep the forecasts in your room and simply test suitable friends when they come along. As in all previous experiments, decide *in advance* how many you are going to test. We suggest that five is enough, though of course you may do as many as you like.

Results

As before, you can now complete the Astrology Results Sheet, add up the number correct and see whether your result is significant – two right out of four, or three right out of (up to) 14 trials. This is a better test and, if you get a significant result, it suggests that astrology really does work.

Further Experiments

Can you still think of any problems with the controlled test? One of the fun things about science is that you can always make better and better experiments. In this case some psychologists have argued that people nowadays know what their sun signs are supposed to be like, and so they could choose the right forecast that way.

For example, suppose that one of the forecasts said 'with your impulsive but brave nature you are likely to get into trouble this month...' Many people know that Leos are supposed to be impulsive and brave, so they would pick the right one.

How can you guard against this? It is a worrying problem because, if true, it suggests that people all over the place are conforming to what they think they should be like! Perhaps astrology does not really work at all, but because everyone thinks it does they all go around behaving more like their sun signs than they really are. Mothers and fathers who are interested in astrology might even influence their children to grow up according to what their sun sign says they should be like.

One way to test this is to do the experiment without using sun signs. You could get a real astrologer to draw up the horoscope for a number of your friends. Or you might get a computer astrology programme that uses a lot more information than just the sun sign; these are becoming more and more widely available, and some can be run on home computers.

If astrology really works this method should produce better results. In other words, people should find it easier to pick their own forecast because it was based on their exact birthday and time. If astrology is not true they should do worse at this test, because they can no longer rely on the crude distinctions made by the popular astrology of sun signs.

Conclusion

Do you think astrology works? If you have done one or more of the experiments you should have a much better idea than when you started. Draw your own conclusions and make up your own mind. In the future, will you treat astrology as just a bit of fun or as a serious way of learning about your life?

This is the great thing about doing your own science. You don't have to take someone else's word for things. Next time you hear someone make a fantastic claim you will be able to assess it for yourself. Is this a wonderful new idea that will change science and the world for the better? Or is it just a load of old rubbish? You can devise the experiments, and then do them to find the answer.

Index

36459616R00136

Printed in Great Britain
by Amazon